Quiverful

A Compendium of Reflections, Meditations, Convictions,
Questions, One-Liners, Jokes, Arguments,

concerning the exploration of human sexuality,

with the conversations particularly in mind
between those of different sexual dispositions,

for their encouragement
and for the sharpening of their arrows

as they engage with those willing to listen and respond
in their families
among their co-workers
in their churches
among their friends

by

JIM COTTER

Cairns Publications
Sheffield

in association with

Arthur James
John Hunt Publishing
New Alresford
1999

© Jim Cotter 1999

ISBN 1 90301 918 4

CAIRNS PUBLICATIONS
47 Firth Park Avenue, Sheffield, S5 6HF
In association with
ARTHUR JAMES
An imprint of
JOHN HUNT PUBLISHING
46a West Street, New Alresford,
Hampshire, SO24 9AU, United Kingdom

Further copies of this book
and other Cairns Publications
can be obtained from New Alresford

A catalogue record for this book is available
from the British Library

Printed in Great Britain

CONTENTS

Other books by Jim Cotter

Prayer at Night's Approaching
Prayer at Day's Dawning

Prayer in the Morning
Prayer in the Day

A new unfolding of the Psalms in three volumes:
Through Desert Places
By Stony Paths
Towards the City

Healing - More or Less
Reflections and prayers at the end of an age

Pleasure, Pain and Passion
Some perspectives on sexuality and spirituality

Yes...Minister?
Patterns of Christian service

No Thank You, I'm 1662
Cartoons at the giving of the Peace
(With Stuart Yerrell)

Love Rekindled
Practising hospitality

Love Re-membered
Resources for a House Eucharist

Brainsquall
Soundings from a deep depression

Dazzling Darkness
Cairns for a journey

PREFACE

From time to time, the author has felt, 'Been here before,' and 'Here we go again.' When you have been living with and thinking through a particular human concern for nearly two generations, you do yawn from time to time. But the debates about human sexuality, in particular those about same-sex relationships, are not yet over and the conflicts have not yet been resolved - either for people or for policies. And even an old-timer occasionally surprises himself with a new image, is given a new perspective, laughs at a new joke, and is encouraged by the way in which younger generations are building on the work done in the earlier years of this century: in their turn they are becoming more mature role models for their successors currently in the cradle.

Which brings me to the title of this book. Miles Coverdale's great translation of the Psalms included these lines, Psalm 127.5-6a:

'Like as the arrows in the hand of the giant:

even so are the young children.

Happy is the man that hath his quiver full of them ...'

Doubtless, in their generation, the men were happier the more the quiver was full of sons - though Anthony Trollope was fairer in his description of the fourteen children of Mr and Mrs Quiverful in *Barchester Towers*.

Well, for a writer, the arrows, the children, are the words that flow from the pen, and this book has amore than three hundred of them - if you are willing to regard each day's contribution as a lively offspring.

The image of the arrow, however, is 'nearer the mark' for the purpose of these 'thoughts for the day'. I hope that many of them are sharp enough for resounding hits at their targets, their feathers all a-quiver. Issues around human sexuality provoke passionate arguments, and some of these arrows may make their 'point' with 'sharpness'. They are not intended to give permanent wounds. But we all learn from the kind of remark that makes us say, 'Ouch. That one went home.' (However, the author cannot guarantee that any of these arrows will be from Cupid's bow...)

It may also be worth remembering that visions and mirages quiver in the heat. Certainly waves of energy have been set in motion for the writer by the shaping of these words. It is up to the reader to discern whether they mislead or clarify.

JIM COTTER
Sheffield, July 1999

A SPIRITUAL HEALTH WARNING

A note from the author and compiler of this compendium:
Writers delve deep
to discover words that make sense
and help them to resolve inner conflicts
that they do not know how to resolve in action.
They rarely practise what they preach.
They are more likely to be wise in word than in deed.
If we should meet,
beware.
Don't expect too much of me.
We shall both be starting at the beginning,
all over again...

A NOTE ON TREES

How many trees have been used to publish this book? Well, only the pulp is used, which comes from the trimmings: the trunks are used for furniture. A commercially grown softwood tree produces, on average, about one-sixth of a ton of pulp. Since this book has used about one ton, it has needed six trees to produce it - but of course not all of those six trees. By weight it has needed about three-quarters of one tree. So John Hunt Publishing and Cairns Publications are donating the wherewithal for the planting of two trees, in gratitude and recompense.

A NOTE ON SOURCES

At the bottom of some of the pages that follow you will see the word 'Source'. If the text has inverted commas anywhere in it, that indicates a direct quotation, and the necessary acknowledgments are listed.

If there are no inverted commas, this indicates that the author has been inspired and encouraged by the Source that is named, but has woven his own thoughts around it.

Usually the item is a mixture of précis and comment. Sometimes the various strands are impossible to separate, but the author and not the Source is responsible for the words and ideas expressed. There are a few instances where he has not been able to look up the original to check whether or not he has unwittingly quoted, so much has that original been absorbed over the years. If direct quotations have not been acknowledged, he apologizes: corrections will be made in any future edition. And his thanks in this instance for the kick starts - or nudge starts.

Also he has drawn on many conversations the details of which he has forgotten, and has been nurtured over the long haul by embracings both tentative and full-bodied. Again, gratitude.

A few pages have been lifted, some directly, from two previous books by the author, *Good Fruits:* Same-sex relationships and Christian faith, and *Pleasure, Pain, and Passion:* Some reflections on sexuality and spirituality. *Good Fruits*, with its two editions in 1981 and 1988, is now out of print. It consisted of a selection of articles in a series called 'Our God Too' in *Gay News* in the late seventies, together with a selection of longer essays and addresses.

This book, the bulk of which is new, is its successor, But the format of a 'thought for the day', with its discipline of a maximum of 200 words per page, has both concentrated the mind and led to a considerable re-working of what had become, in tone if not in theme, somewhat dated.

HOW TO USE THIS BOOK

There are three ways in which the material in this book might be used.

The first is straightforwardly, chapter by chapter.

The second is as 'thoughts for the day', following the dates as they are indicated at the bottom of each page.

The third is as a collection of resources on which you can draw in different circumstances. So, if you want

the light touch, look up chapter 3;

material for debate, look up chapters 4-8, 10;

material for prayer, look up chapter 11;

material for blessings of same-sex parterships, look up chapter 11;

approaches to the Bible, look up chapter 1;

encouragement, look up chapters 2, 12, 13.

A NOTE ON COPYRIGHT

Author and publisher positively invite you to quote from this book and to make copies of selections of it for educational or religious purposes. A specific copyright fee is requested only when material is being copied for commercial purposes. But we do ask that

1. you make a clear acknowledgment of the source, listing author, title, publisher, year of publication, and page number(s);

2. you make no alteration to the text without consulting the author first: you may well be suggesting an improvement - which will be gratefully received - but there may be a reason for the wording that is not obvious but is important to the overall meaning;

3. you tell us about the occasion and which passage(s) you are using: such information is appreciated, not least in the planning of future work.

4. you consider sending a donation for the work of the Lesbian and Gay Christian Movement or the Woodland Trust.

1
CONSULTING ANCESTORS

Peter Tatchell writes:
   'I ... was reading Leviticus 20.13 where it says
   that homosexuals should be put to death.
   Over the centuries,
   millions of gay people have been stoned to death,
   burnt alive and hanged from the gallows
   as a result of the Bible's teaching.
   The Bible is to gays what Mein Kampf is to Jews.'

Ouch.
Come off it, you can't treat the Bible like that.
Only a literalist would read it in that way.

But of course that's the problem.
That is exactly the way that the Bible has been read
   by most people for most of the past two thousand years.

I may want to approach it differently -
   you know, more sophisticated than thou -
many of the readers of this book may wish to do likewise.
I suspect Peter Tatchell knows that!

But he's right:
   THE BIBLE, heavyweight,
   has been and still is used to bash,
   and if it is not used directly to kill,
   it can still be used to create an atmosphere
   which gives people permission to be violent,
   and this does lead to murder.

Witness the killing of Matthew Shepard,
   a gay student in Wyoming in 1998 ...
Witness the internalized condemnation
   of gay teenagers rejected by their parents
   and subsequently committing suicide ...

Source: Peter Tatchell, *The Guardian*, 27 January 1999

Beware when someone begins,
  'The Bible says ...'
You can usually expect the person
  either to be avoiding personal antagonism
  or to be avoiding thought
    or both.

It looks easy,
  this believing that every word in the Bible
  is both true and of equal value -
  and that such truths are obvious.

In practice,
  most of those who turn to the Bible
  (including those of us who are not literalists)
  select some texts and ignore others,
  and find themselves falling into the habit
  of returning to some passages
  much more frequently than to others.

Personally,
  I get on with Luke better than Matthew,
    John better than Paul,
    Jacob and Job better than Leviticus and Ezra.
  And so on.
I don't mean by this that I find what they have to say
  congenial or easy,
    more that I can accept challenges from some people
      more than I can from others.
  I'd rather be put on the spot by certain bishops
    of the present day than by others.
I'll resist naming any more names ...

A well-thumbed Bible
  is usually well-thumbed only in parts.
You can tell by looking how worn and coloured
  the bottom edge of the paper is.

I think literalists forget

    that a living community is always more important
      than anything written down ...

    that the person whose Bible bears a sticker
      with the words 'Maker's Instructions'
        is believing in an eighteenth and nineteenth century
         sort of way,
      which imagined
        God as a clockmaker,
      devising engineering blueprints,
        with every detail of a machine
        worked out in advance ...

that writers are not mechanics
    writing at supposed heavenly dictation ...

that their work is more imaginative
    and engaging than that ...

that the kind of God we believe in
    is surely not less than personal -
and to take down dictation
    is not the most creative thing a human being does
      with a pen ...

that God calls each of us
    to be persons, not channels -
      again another impersonal picture -
    and takes the risk
      that we won't get everything right -
        not even in work that we come to regard
         as Scriptures.

The atmosphere will be safer if someone begins,

> The writer of this particular book of the Bible
>   was expressing what he or his contemporaries
>   (even possibly she or her contemporaries)
>   understood what God was revealing to them
>   as they struggled with their contemporary
>   pressures and circumstances and puzzles.

And we might find what they wrote
    to be helpful to us in our contemporary debates,
    as we engage in conversation with them,
    as we struggle with new knowledge
    and new pressures and circumstances.

This is what a Living Tradition is all about:
    each generation participates,
    honouring the ancestors,
    but not following them slavishly,
    making its own contribution,
    and helping to maintain the 'Momentum'.

Some will temperamentally want to slow the train down:
    if they have everything their way,
    inertia sets in and the train stops.
Some will temperamentally want to speed the train up:
    if they have everything their way,
    the train comes off the rails.
But there is no way we can avoid arguments,
    even among skilled drivers.

The Bible is not a series of bland reports.
It is more a matter of
    There's never a dull moment with God
and
    You ain't seen nothing yet ...

Five things to remember when examining ancient law codes
to avoid transferring them directly to the present day:

1 They are a snapshot from one particular time.
   They could be and often were changed.
       (According to Leviticus 20.10 both adulterer
       and adulteress were to be put to death,
       according to John 8.5 the law was that only
       the adulteress should be so punished.)

2 They are set in the context of a whole book
   with its own particular theology.

3 The book itself is set in the context of the Bible,
   the whole having a number of layers of
   interpretation and discernment.

4 They are part of a symbolic system
   which no longer applies to any of us:
   e.g. we think of body discharges differently.

5 They do not have a decisive part to play
   in any Christian thinking.

NB Dogs and the sea both have a bad press in the Bible.
       Watch out Crufts and P&O.
       (And of course therefore,
       Christians never go cruising ...)

Source: Michael Vasey, *Strangers and Friends*, Hodder and Stoughton, 1995

The Bible is a very disturbing book
  if you are timid and conventional.
God is quite cavalier with the laws about sex
  which are supposed to have originated
  with Him.
(And the God of the Bible is very much
  Him with a capital H.)
God's purposes are believed to have been
  enacted by people who break the rules.

Perhaps because King David was no paragon
  the writers were careful to surround his ancestry
  with doubtful deeds.
After all, Solomon was born because David was
  overwhelmed by Bathsheba and conveniently
  had her husband Uriah killed at the front.
And he had had a dodgy relationship as a young man
  with King Saul's son Jonathan,
  which was certainly passionate and physical
  and intensely loyal,
  (each carried on his person a piece of the other's
    clothing),
  and was a threat to the dynasty.
And younger sons are not supposed to be all that
  favoured by patriarchs:
they can cause a deal of trouble.
But David was the youngest,
  as was the slithery Jacob,
  and others that could be mentioned.

[contd. on the next page]

And what about Tamar?
  She disguised herself as a prostitute
  and slept with her *father-in-law*,
  and one of the resultant twins
  was one of King David's ancestors.
Then there was the *Moabite* Ruth
  (which made her suspect anyway),
  who 'clung' to her *Israelite* mother-in-law Naomi,
  (the verb is the same as that used
  of man and woman who become one flesh),
  and the two powerless childless widows
  conspire to trap Boaz into a marriage
  from whose lineage came David.

Not that everything unusual concerns David.
Eunuchs are to be especially favoured
  according to Isaiah 56,
and they can't exactly do their duty.
And the Song of Songs gives no hint
  that the passionate love it describes
  is married love.
And it is a *mutual* love,
  which is both hard to establish under patriarchy
  and against the rules:
you can tell it is mutual because
  you often do not know
  if it is the man or the woman who is speaking.
And it celebrates desire, not fertility.

Patriarchy still wins as a system,
  but it seems as if God is frequently subversive
  of His own system.
Perhaps it's not so universal after all ...

[contd. from previous page]

Much is made in church circles of the statement that
  'the two become one flesh'.
It is part of the accounts of creation in Genesis,
  and is often used to defend the 'normality'
  of heterosexual marriage.
It is important to be clear that
  it is *not* a statement about sex.
It is about the establishing of a new kinship group,
  of a new unit in society,
one that also creates an alliance between two families.
They did not even conceive
  of the bonding of two people
  in an essentially private relationship of love,
  in which the families of each
  may have little or nothing to do with each other.
If the quotation challenges us at all,
  in both heterosexual and homosexual relationships,
it is whether we have privatized our relationships too far,
  that we are happier about subsuming them
  as a particular kind of the general category of friendship
than as relationships that are
  recognized by law,
  celebrated by public rites of passage,
  instrumental in significantly, if subtly, altering
    everybody else's relationship with the couples
    concerned.

David and Jonathan:

Plenty of homoerotic desire in the story.
    Remember that in their day
    such desire could run parallel with marriage
    not as an alternative to it.

David's lament at hearing of Jonathan's death
    is one of the most beautiful and moving
    in all literature.
It is clear that their relationship was among the
    most significant in David's life,
and that it could be publicly mourned.

It was also publicly acknowledged
    through the covenant that they made together.
Such friendships did not belong to the private sphere alone
    but were a new kinship:
David refers to 'my brother Jonathan'.

The cultural context is of the devotion of heroes.
    Such love is not inconsistent with military valour.

King Saul disapproved because the friendship
    was taking Jonathan away from his responsibility
    to continue the male line.

The theological component of the story
    is that God moves through the unusual and the marginal
    to further His purposes.
The choice of a shepherd boy to be king
    and an unorthodox love
are both signs of God's activity.
Not many conservative Christians are comfortable
    with that thought.

Sources: 1 Samuel 14, 18. 1-5; 2 Samuel 1.17-27

Genesis 19.1-29 and the similar account in Judges 19-21:
   What do we make of this classic Sodom story,
   with its threat to the well-being of visitors?

Some people dismiss the sexual element in it,
   and focus on the inhospitality.
But in the story the sexual is the focus,
   the particular way inhospitality is exercised.
So, looking precisely at what is described as happening:

1   Sexually, it is attempted gang rape of strangers
              by laddish inhabitants of the town,
         apparently heterosexual males
              intent on humiliation,
         violating the laws of hospitality,
              and treating guests 'like women',
              thus de-masculinizing them.

2   Lot's desperate tactic:
              It is better - by his understanding of the law -
              to offer his daughters to these lustful men
              than to offend against his tradition of hospitality.

Whatever the motifs for the time,
   for us there are at least two questions:

1   Would you wish to denigrate women?
         The ancient world may have assumed
              that men were always dominant and superior,
              and that women were their property,
         but is that your assumption?

2   Would you wish to denigrate sexuality
              by assuming that all same-sex activity
              is morally equivalent to rape?

Deuteronomy 23.17-18

The context is hardly that of present-day relationships.
Sacred prostitution was characteristic of fertility cults:
   to engage in it was to put into practice your belief
     that land and people would consequently
      be more fruitful.
The Israelites were against the practice,
   claiming it an 'abomination' and 'idolatry'.
It was not so much that the *sex* was wrong,
   more the *religious* practice of which sex was a part
   that was offensive.
And if that was the only context in which homosexual acts
  were thought to take place,
no wonder there was a blanket prohibition by law,
   as we read in Leviticus 18.22 and 20.13.

But why an 'abomination'?

1   Male dignity was thought to be compromised
          when a man acted 'like a woman'.
        Note that nothing in Leviticus mentions
          sexual acts between women.
2   The distaste and disgust, then as now,
          that people have for acts that are foreign to them.
        acts that are perceived and rejected as 'unclean'.
3   Most important, the pre-scientific understanding
          that semen contains the entire new human being,
          and that the woman is the passive recipient,
          the 'soil' in which the 'seed' is planted.
        So the spilling of the seed by coitus interruptus,
          by male homosexual acts, by male masturbation,
          is tantamount to abortion and murder.

So the unambiguous command of the Hebrew Scriptures
   is to execute men who commit homosexual acts.

Some questions:

1 Is masturbation a worse sin than rape?
    The Church of the Middle Ages in Europe
    gave a more severe penance for masturbation
    because at least rape might result in conception.

2 Is masturbation a sin in any circumstances?

3 If overpopulation is a threat to human survival,
    might our moral assessment of homosexual acts
    differ from those ancient circumstances
    in which a particular tribe was struggling
    to secure its hold on new territory,
    outnumbered by surrounding hostile tribes?

4 Should people be judged on the basis of disgust?

5 If a society's rules do not even mention women
    in the context of homosexuality,
and if all the rules are made by men
    and favour men,
should we regard such rules as prescriptions
    valid for all time?

Leviticus 18.19,29; 15.19-24

What about these ancient laws about menstruation?

When blood flowed out of a human body,
   the person was thereby rendered
     'ritually unclean',
   not simply unclean in the sense
     that there was a bit of a mess to clear up.

Intercourse made you unclean until sunset,
   menstruation made a women unclean for seven days.
Therefore no sex during menstruation.

The penalty was 'kareth',
   'to be cut off from your people'.
This meant execution by stoning, burning, or strangling,
   or, if you were relatively fortunate,
   flogging or expulsion from the community.

Would you say that heterosexual intercourse
   during menstruation was wrong
   and should be similarly punished today?

It is not unknown to this day
   for periods to be known as 'the curse',
   though some have come to think of them
     as a 'wise wound' ...

Deuteronomy 22.13-21, 22

Adultery is defined by the marital status of the woman.
A man cannot commit adultery against his own wife,
   but only against another man
   by having intercourse with that man's wife.
The punishment is stoning to death
   of both man and woman.

So also for a bride found not to be a virgin -
   but *male* virginity is not even mentioned.

The reason?

Fathers have to do their best to make sure
   their children are theirs,
especially if marriage is primarily about
   property and inheritance.
Now fathers can never be 100% sure -
   unlike mothers -
   who are *always* 100% sure -
   unless of course an artificial procedure is used.
So women are treated as property to be owned,
   and, if necessary, controlled and policed.

Adultery is therefore an act of trespass
   against another man's property.

But, of course, the Bible says ...

NB   Adultery may still be wrong,
        but on what grounds now?

What about a man having many wives -
   or concubines?
(We would call such practices polygamy
   and cohabitation.)

The Bible does not give us a picture of a woman
   with many husbands or concubines:
this reinforces the suspicion
   that it is almost entirely written *by* men *to* men.

Polygamy and cohabitation are *regular* practices
   that are not condemned in the Hebrew Scriptures.
The three references in the New Testament
   are not comprehensively or structurally critical:
there is the simple instruction that bishops, deacons,
   and elders are to have only one wife.
See 1 Timothy 3.2,12 and Titus 1.6.

Yes, a man and a woman become 'one flesh',
   according to the understanding of Genesis 2.24,
   creating a new social unit,
but nowhere in the Hebrew Scriptures is this taken to mean
   the exclusion of other partners.

Jesus refers to Genesis in his comments about marriage,
   but is not specifically critical of the *structure*
   of these other arrangements.
(We may wish to draw out that implication,
   but that is to do something different
   from simply relying on what the Bible says -
   or in this case doesn't say.)
Polygamy continued to be practised in Judaism
   for centuries after the time of Jesus.
Mormons and other Christian groups
   have not found the Bible clear and unambiguous.

Nudity can still cause us embarrassment and shame.
Contrast the naturist's beach with towel contortionists.
Contrast nudity in the privacy of one's home
   with the humiliation of having one's jeans removed.

In ancient Israel *all* nudity in *all* circumstances was taboo,
   not simply in the shaming of prisoners and enemies.
See Isaiah 20.2-4, 2 Samuel 10.4-5, Isaiah 47.2-3.

To demonstrate that the Canaanites were inferior,
   the writer of Genesis 9.20-27 told the story of Ham,
   patriarchal ancestor of the Canaanites,
   who saw his father Noah naked in his tent.
As punishment, Ham and his descendants
   were to become as slaves to his brothers.

It is hard to believe that the taboo was never broken,
   especially in the intimacies of lovers.
After all, the writer of the Song of Songs
   must have seen something!
Yet the taboo has remained powerful into modern times,
   even between husbands and wives.
And as well as the taboo we suffer from the distortion
   that what we see in the mirror is not lovable,
   and that the body is inferior to the soul.

Do we continue to be influenced by such regulations
   because they are in the Bible?
Do we need anything more than a law against
   deliberately causing public offence?
And what does that cover?
   Streaking across a football pitch during a match?
   A striptease in a night club?
   Making love at midnight in a forest glade?
Again, ask the question,
Is there a difference between 'in public'
   and 'in a public place'?

In 1 Samuel 24.3 in the King James version of the Bible
   we read that Saul went into a cave
   'to cover his feet'.
This is a literal translation from the Hebrew,
   and it is also a euphemism.
It does not mean that Saul had sore feet
   and went into the cave to put his sandals on.
It means that he went into the cave to squat,
   one consequence being that
     his flowing outer garment covered his feet,
   the other that he,
     as most modern translations put it,
      'relieved himself'.

(The first edition of an American translation,
   The Living Bible, substituted another euphemism:
Saul went into the cave to go to the bathroom.
Pardon?
Have archaeologists made a discovery
   I haven't heard about?)

On the whole we now prefer plain speaking to euphemism.
Or do we still think we can be 'soiled' and 'tainted' if we
   use certain 'dirty' words?
And in a book I can write 'genitals'
   without a second thought,
but if I used more everyday expressions
   this book might not find its ways
   on to the shelves of - er - respectable bookshops ...

(If I am writing prayers I definitely become
   poetic and old-fashioned,
   and write 'loins' ...)

Excuse me while I take what Americans call
   'a senior moment',
   and laugh ...

Patterns of sexual behaviour vary:

1   The Song of Songs contains poems that celebrate
       erotic love, not married love.

2   Proof of fertility *before* marriage
       has been required in some societies,
       especially where the lack of children
       would mean financial hardship.

3   Prostitution has been regarded as a social necessity
       which protects the virginity of other women
       and the property rights of husbands
       (safeguarding their wives
       from predatory single men).
     See Genesis 38.12-19 and Joshua 2.1-7.
     Note that men were not regarded as sinners,
       only the prostitutes.
     Plus ça change ...

Which of these three forms of extra-marital sex
   would you disapprove of?
And why?

After all, you can find them in the Bible ...

'When men fight with one another,
   and the wife of the one draws near
   to rescue her husband
   from the hand of him who is beating him,
   and puts out her hand
   and seizes him by the private parts,
   then you shall cut off her hand;
   your eye shall have no pity.'

Thus Deuteronomy 25.11-12.

Well, *that's* a tricky verse for literalists.

Certainly the old biblical writers did not flinch
   from the most vivid descriptions of violence.

Definitely a passage to be read
   only after the nine o'clock watershed.

What, no applause that she was bravely intervening
   to save her husband's life?

(Presumably the argument would have been
   that the woman could have damaged
   the sower's ability to sow his seed-
   or oats.)

Celibacy is abnormal -
   according to the Bible.
Compulsory celibacy is heretical -
   according to 1 Timothy 4.1-3
   (it is wrong to forbid marriage).
It may be a vocation for a few,
   but should it be imposed on a category,
  e.g. clergy?

If God intends men and women to marry
   and have children,
is it wrong - or second-class - to be
   celibate by vocation?
   single by circumstances?
   childless by choice?
   homosexual by desire?

Heterosexual marriage may be normal -
   statistically speaking:
this does not thereby make it normative -
   universally practised -
   ideally speaking.

Paul preferred people to be unmarried -
   as he was.
Paul referred to marriage as a divine gift,
   a calling,
   not simply the natural way.
See 1 Corinthians 7.7.

Where do you stand on these issues?

The question is hardly answerable simply with,
   The Bible says ...

Some societies have leant on the Bible
  to forbid marrying anyone
  outside your tribal group or race.
Israelites were not to marry Canaanites -
  or anyone else that was not Jewish.

Until recently mixed marriages were forbidden
  in the southern states of America:
the dominant Southern Baptist Church
  quoted the Bible in support.

Similarly,
  ... in South Africa ... Dutch Reformed Church ...

Verses in the New Testament declare
  that there are no social separations in Christ.
But this conviction has in practice
  been spiritualized, not socialized:
we may be united in Christ, but not in law.

Yet the biblical writings -
  especially among the prophets -
  are shot through with a passion for social justice.

Just because our ancestors did not act upon
  all the implications of their faith
does not mean that we should endorse those limitations.

To do so would be wilfully obtuse.

Slavery is a parallel issue.

The biblical writers took the *institution* of slavery
  as a social norm.
Personal relationships between master and slave
  may occasionally have been transformed
  because both were *in Christ*,
but slavery as such was never condemned.

Male *owners* of slaves could do what they liked with them:
  they had power of life and death over them.

Female slaves, along with concubines and captives,
  could be
    sexual playthings,
    breeding machines,
    involuntary wives.
See 2 Samuel 5.13, Judges 19-21, Numbers 31.18.

Such a perspective, mindset, and practice
  were typical of the American South 150 years ago -

because the Bible told them so ...

It's unnatural.
It's a grave offence.
It's universally condemned in the Bible.
It's condemned by
    Augustine in the days of the early Church,
    Thomas Aquinas in the Middle Ages,
    Martin Luther, sixteenth-century German Protestant,
    Richard Hooker, sixteenth-century Anglican.

Between 1550 and 1650 all the churches of Europe
    totally changed their minds.
The practice was the lending of money at interest,
    especially condemned when the rate was excessive.
It could be tolerated
    (because commercially useful)
    among Jews in medieval Europe,
    (dirty money),
    but not practised among Christians.

Well, are you now going to withdraw your money
    from bank or building society?

Perhaps we should,
    perhaps lending money at interest
    is a structural, systemic injustice ...

And that would be to change our minds again ...

NB   What was changing in the sixteenth century was
            the way in which money was understood,
        that it was not simply a matter of
            you have more if I have less,
            but that it could *grow*.

Homosexual acts are mentioned three times
  in the New Testament.

1 Corinthians 6.9 and 1 Timothy 1.10
  probably have in mind
  'passive' and 'active' partners in anal sex.
The context is unclear,
  most likely paper tissue sex or sex for money.

Romans 1.26-27 condemns *heterosexual* men and women
for 'leaving', 'giving up', 'exchanging'
  what was 'normal' and 'natural'
  for an 'aberration' and 'abomination'.

His aim was laudable enough,
  to show that no human being has rights over God
  and to lead human beings
  to harmonious relationships with one another
    and with God.

It was not his fault that he was unaware
  that to have homosexual desires
  is normal and natural
  for a proportion of the population
  in every society yet known.
He knew nothing of same-sex relationships
  which have mutual love and respect at their centre.
Today he might well expand his understanding
  of what is natural.

Perhaps at the deepest level,
  we have to ask again,
is there a heterosexual blueprint for human sexuality
  given once and for all at the beginning of creation,
or is creation an ongoing dynamic process,
  allowing for change and variety?

You may be *rationally* persuaded that the Scriptures
  cannot be used to condemn all forms
  of homosexual behaviour,
you may be persuaded by the argument
  that our knowledge and perception have changed,
  that our discernment now needs to be exercised
  between life-enhancing and death-dealing actions,
you may know in your mind
  that it is too simple to fall back on
  The Bible says ...

Yet you may still be *emotionally* gripped by the old words,
  hearing the stern, condemning voices
  of preachers, teachers, judges, and parents,
  as well as the mocking scorn of your peers
  and the 'praying-against-you' of congregations.
You may still see the pointed finger
  and the fanatical gleam of the eye.

Four recommendations:

1   Don't read those passages ever again!
       You will only feed the hostile energy
         that comes your way from them.

2   If you can't avoid hearing them read, remember
         that you are a living, contributing member
           of the continuing, developing tradition of faith;
         that our ancestors were struggling to do right
           in the light of what they knew;
         that they could often be wrong;
         that new knowledge alters our approach.

3   Nourish yourself with positive biblical insights
         that have stood the test of time.
       Read the rest of this chapter.

4   Don't forget to laugh.

Rules about sexual behaviour
   are viewed in the whole Bible
   as moral commandments.
If we regard the Bible as in any way important,
   they have to be taken *seriously*.
We have to give them our considered attention.

But we have two problems:
One, not even literalists actually treat every verse
   in the Bible as of equal merit.
Two, most people who do take the Bible seriously
   disagree about which rules are binding.

How do you decide?
What is your principle of selection?

The next few pages give one person's list of
   agreements and disagreements.

Ask yourself if you in turn agree or disagree.

But first, reflect on that basic question,

How do you decide when faced with dilemmas
   about how to act?

I agree with the Bible in rejecting

Incest

Rape

Adultery

Intercourse with animals

I would bring in considerations like these:

Do my actions make me and others
  less or more human?
To be more human is to be just and loving
  in my use of power -
and there is quite a lot about that in the Bible.

  I would seek to exclude violence -
    better, violation -
    in all my actions
      (while not being self-righteous in claiming
      that I always succeed).

I would argue against adultery
  in terms of a betrayal of a binding covenant
    (therefore in terms of the quality of the relationship
    rather than on grounds of men owning women
      as their property,
    with adultery seen as an act of trespass).

I do not agree with the Bible in rejecting

Intercourse during menstruation

Celibacy, when freely embraced as a vocation

Homosexual acts in all circumstances

Marrying someone of another race or religion

Explicit naming of sexual organs

Nudity

Masturbation

Birth control

Semen and menstrual blood as offensive, unclean,
and taboo

I sometimes avoid Anglo-Saxon words
out of courtesy,
as a matter of taste,
or as a joke,
but not as a matter of divine command.
(He's a 'friend friend' not a 'euphemism friend'.)

I would except nudity
in public places where it would give offence,
in private places where it would be tasteless.
Anyway I am firmly convinced
a certain amount of clothing enhances the erotic,
while nothing at all often deadens it.

Masturbation, rarely, can become obsessive,
the person lacking the ability and energy for intimacy.

I do not agree with the Bible in permitting
　　(or at least not clearly rejecting)

Prostitution
　　(but because it is symptomatic
　　　　of male control
　　　　of *systemic* poverty
　　　　and of treating person as thing)

Polygamy
　　and, (though the Bible never mentions it)
　　polyandry

Marrying your dead husband's brother -
　　or, in sequence if necessary, brothers -
　　to secure the continuation of the family line

Sex with slaves
　　(or, indeed, slavery)

Keeping any number of concubines
　　(or any at all -
　　though not all questions about cohabitation
　　are thereby answered)

Treating women as property

Very early marriage,
　　i.e. as soon as reproduction is biologically possible.

I accept divorce with realistic reluctance,
　　not on grounds of adultery alone,
　　but on grounds of irretrievable breakdown
　　　　of the relationship.
The people of Jesus's day accepted divorce
　　at the whim of the husband.
Jesus rejected it completely,
　　not least thereby enhancing the status of women.

So,

rules are necessary,
purity codes are found everywhere
　　(though operating in different ways
　　in different cultures),
both can and do change -

with, some would wish to add,
　　due attention to
　　and seeking the guidance of
　　　　'Holy Spirit',
a personal presence that is
　　spirit and not letter of the law
and
　　the spirit of wisdom
　　giving us the discernment to recognize
　　fresh and more comprehensive understanding
　　of what is true and right.

The story of the man born blind:
  What caused it? Whose fault?

Different people had different assumptions:
The man and his parents:
  It's a fact of life.
The religious establishment:
  It's an indication that he has nothing to teach the
  community about God.
Jesus:
  It's an indication that because he is an outcast,
  he is specially loved by God.
Those around:
  Embarrassing if you are challenged to change your mind
  in reponse to 'new sight'.

The question of cause fades into irrelevance.

What matters is the change from being
  a reject from society
to being
  a friend of God.

It is not that the blind need curing
  if they are to know God.
They need a healing community
  which lives counter to the web
  of social and religious oppression
  in which we are all caught.

Certain parallels suggest themselves ...

Source: John 9, with commentary by Michael Vasey, *Strangers and Friends*,
Hodder and Stoughton, 1995

The centurion and his 'pais'.

This is one of the healing stories told about Jesus.

Notice that he welcomes a figure of military authority,
  one who is instrumental in the oppression of Israel.

Notice that he commends his degree of faith as unusual.

Notice that there is no criticism of the centurion's deep
  concern for his 'pais'.

English Bibles usually translate 'pais' as 'servant'.

It is more accurately translated 'boy':
  yes, it is a standard term for a servant
  (it was commonly used in the British Empire
  and in apartheid South Africa
  by white masters to call their coloured servants);
but it was also an affectionate diminutive
  that indicated a sexual relationship.

It was characteristic of the early churches
  that personal relationships of deep affection
    did much to soften the harshness
    of the structures of power:
  the patriarch in relation to women and to the young;
  the owner in relation to slaves;
  the imperial power in relation to the colonies.

Such personal relationships were also a standing rebuke
  to those power structures,
and although those with power
  might bend the rules at times,
  they made sure that the rules remained the same.

Sources: Matthew 8:5-13, Luke 7:1-10; Philemon

Jesus and friendship

He and the disciples formed a same sex social grouping.
Such associations were by no means unusual
   and were acceptable.

Friendship itself was respected:
   it was egalitarian but also a social bond;
   affectionate intimacy was at its heart,
   and its erotic potential was not suspect.

It is reported that the 'disciple whom he loved'
   lay close to him at the Last Supper.

It is reported that he no longer wished to call his
   followers servants but friends.

It is reported that he had the gift of intimate touch
   with all who came to him in need,
   not least the outcasts.

And if 'love' is an all-purpose and often weasel word,
   it includes and even binds together
   the 'agape' of unselfish goodwill,
   the 'philia' of affection,
   and the 'eros' of passionate desire.
There is no reason to suppose that for Jesus
   the energies of friendship excluded 'eros'.

Of course, the Church has more often been
   a moral police force
   or an arm of state power
   or a model for families
than an agency for friendships.

The biblical notion of marriage is close to slavery -
  at least it was for women.
The story of Hosea is of his faithfulness
  towards his wife who had left him
and so of God's faithfulness towards Israel.
Both God and husband are very jealous.
And what does the husband propose
  in order to retrieve his errant wife?
He threatens her ...
He prevents her reaching her lovers ...
He considers seduction ...
Whatever happens, he will remain in control.
Hardly the mutuality that the churches
  finally caught up with:
see the Marriage Service in the
  Alternative Service Book of the Church of England
and the document *Gaudium et Spes*
  of the Second Vatican Council.

Whoever wrote the letters to the Ephesians
  and Colossians, Paul or someone in his circle,
we find the language of authority over others,
and in marriage the man having the power and rights
  over his wife.
Wives must submit, be subject to, obey -
  exactly as children and slaves must.
Doubtless there was much personal kindness,
  but as with slavery the institutions of society
  acted as a constantly intrusive context.
Again, this is not a model for today
  that many would wish to adopt.

Sources: Hosea 1-3, Ephesians 5:22-25, 28, Colossians 3:18-20,22

Translators often reflect their own pre-suppositions
   and also have to deal with the pre-suppositions
   of the original writers.
There is much room for blunder and confusion.

Take two contentious words in 1 Corinthians 6.9-10:
   'malakoi' and 'arsenokoitai'.
'Malakoi' is translated
   'effeminate' in the King James Bible and J. B. Phillips,
   'voluptuous persons' in Bagster's Interlinear
      Greek/English translation,
   'male prostitutes' in the New Revised Standard Version,
   'self-indulgent' in the New Jerusalem Bible.
'Arsenokoitai' is translated
   'abusers of themselves with mankind' in the King James
      Bible,
   'sodomites' in Bagster's, the New Revised Standard
      Version, and the New Jerusalem Bible.
Both words are translated together as
   'homosexuals' in the Revised Standard Version,
   'homosexual perversion' in the New English Bible,
   'homosexual perverts' in the Good News Bible,
   'sexual perverts' in the Revised English Bible.

Michael Vasey uses the word 'wanton' for 'malakoi'.
   We probably cannot get anything more accurate than
   'sexual wrongdoing', associated with the perceived
   idolatry and oppression of Roman society,
   with unequal, exploitative, and abusive acts.
There is no hint in either word of loving relationships.
Further, nowhere in biblical literature is Sodom's sin linked
   with what we now call sodomy -
and sodomite is a label that has killed thousands.
And the first four letters of the second word,
   to which the modern eye is drawn, do not help.
As Vasey says, 'Careless exegesis costs lives.'

Source: Michael Vasey, *Strangers and Friends*, Hodder and Stoughton, 1995

If Paul could address us now
   and say what he was getting at in Romans chapter 1,
he might say something like this:

I wanted to demonstrate that all human beings
   fall short of what God intends them to become.
I wanted to show that those of us who were Jewish
   had not kept the Law, either ritual or moral,
and neither had those who were Gentiles,
   who in their own way were also unclean and wicked.

Because there was conflict in our churches
   between those of Jewish background
   and those of Gentile background
(food laws and circumcision were hot topics)
I chose an issue that in our day was not contentious
   simply to make a point in my argument.

It is interesting that you are now hotly debating that issue -
   what you call homosexual acts -
while you have no controversies about the other two!

For those of us with Jewish backgrounds,
   to take part in homosexual acts
   was to betray our very identity as Jews,
   as much as to eat pork or not to be circumcised.
All these things were against our 'nature'.
They were not 'in our character'.
We would not have felt 'complete' or 'proper'
   if we had done them.
It would have been against our customs, our standards...

[contd. on next two pages]

... But when I used the same example with those
   of Gentile background,
I still thought such acts were *unclean*,
   but not necessarily morally *wrong* -
just as it was not necessarily wrong for them
   to eat pork or remain uncircumcised.

Such 'impurity' was *one* of the consequences
   of turning away from God,
   which is what we meant by idolatry.
They were certainly acting against
   what was socially acceptable,
just as Jews would have been,
   taking part in unusual and unexpected acts
   contrary to their customs.
It was degrading
   (de-grading, or socially lowering)
and shameful.
Such uncleanness was the recompense
   they received among themselves.
And all our societies in the Mediterranean world
   were governed by notions of honour and shame.

Now you may have forgotten
   that I had become aware that such 'purity'
   should no longer be a relevant category
   for deciding whether or not a person
   was to be shamed and excluded from the community.
Jesus abolished it.
No action *of itself* was clean or unclean.

Can you imagine how very difficult it was
   for those of us trying to follow Jesus
to act upon that new understanding?

[contd. from previous page and on next page]

... I for one found it easier to change my mind
   about pork and circumcision
   than about certain kinds of sexual acts.
In fact, I was blind to the possibility
   that such acts might not always be wrong.
But at least I did not include them in my list of sins.
In fact there is nothing sexual among them.
And I tried to make it clear
   that wrongdoing was the *second* consequence of idolatry,
   to be distinguished from uncleanness.
My list was a fairly conventional one,
   but important none the less:
covetousness, malice, envy, murder, strife, deceit,
   malignity, gossiping, slander, insolence, hardheartedness,
   ruthlessness, and so on.

As I look at your contemporary situation,
   I can well understand that you still find it easy
   to associate sex with what is dirty and shameful,
that you might well feel ashamed of certain sexual acts,
   your culture still finding them socially unacceptable.
I myself found the very thought disgusting.
But I would claim that I did not use such acts
   as among my list of examples of sins.
And if you go on to ask whether or not
   you should feel guilty,
I think I would want to ask whether or not
   your sexual actions took on any of the character
   of that list of sins.
Are they abusive or exploitative in any way?
If not,
   then, in the Spirit of Jesus,
you must make up your own minds.

[contd. from previous two pages]

Source: Daniel Heminiack, *What the Bible Really Says about Homosexuality*,
Alamo Square Press, San Francisco, 1994, chapter six; and sundry commentaries on that difficult chapter one of Paul's Letter to the Romans

Also remember that Paul

was not a family man;

treated nobody as unclean;

was often tender, gentle, emotional;

had strong emotional relationships
with both women and younger men;

experienced ostracism and desertion
by some of the churches.

He would probably have felt quite at home
in the Lesbian and Gay Christian Movement,
even if there might be some opposition to proposing him
as patron saint ...

Contemporary lesbian and gay people are *with* Paul:
  in condemning the aggressive masculinity of the culture
    (as in Romans 1);
  in welcoming the expression of private affection
    in public places (it was taken for granted in his day);
  in resisting any limitation of emotional and intimate
    relationships to the home (because of his own
    relationships as an unmarried man).
St Paul in the Letter to the Romans
  clearly links homosexual acts with idolatry,
  with turning away from the true God.
Lesbian and gay people in the churches
  serve that true God with distinction and flair.
Their sensibility towards the beautiful
  makes them sensitive to language, music, art,
  to the choreography of bodies,
and this is put at the service of the Mysterious God,
  the Loving God, the Beautiful God.
Their relationships demonstrate in miniature
  this sensibility and sensitivity.
While Paul's argument may have made sense
  in a context of cultic prostitution,
it makes no sense
  in a context either of corporate prayer in the churches
  or of personal relationships in the home.

Rowan Williams criticizes any use of Romans 1
   as the basis for rejecting same-sex relationships.
He imagines a gay man saying that
   he does not experience his sexual desires
   as disordered,
   or doing violence to a (heterosexual) truth already known
   or, consequently, becoming rapacious.

'I want to live in obedience to God;
I truly, prayerfully, and conscientiously
   do not recognize Romans 1
   as describing what I am or what I want.
I am not rejecting something
   I know in the depths of my being.
I struggle against the many inducements
   to live in promiscuous rapacity -
   not without cost.
I do not believe that my identity as a desiring being
   is a complicated and embarrassing extra
   in my humanity as created by God.
And it is hard to hear good news from the Church
   if it insists that my condition
   is in itself spiritually compromised.'

Rowan Williams, 'Knowing myself in Christ', Timothy Bradshaw (ed.), *The Way Forward*, Christian Voices on Homosexuality and the Church, Hodder and Stoughton, 1997, p. 17, reproduced by permission of the publishers.

Rowan Williams goes on to imagine that gay man to say:

'I am not asking just for fulfilment.
I want to know how my human and historical being,
   enacting itself through the negotiation
   of all sorts of varied desires and projects,
   may become transparent to Jesus,
   a sign of the kingdom.
I do not seek to avoid cost.
But for the married,
   that cost is worked out
   in the daily discipline of a shared life,
   which, by the mutual commitment it embodies,
   becomes a means of grace and strength
   for the bearing of the cost.'

Lesbian and gay people are not making a plea
   for a right to self-expression or fulfilment
   or even happiness,
somehow divorced from the rights of others,
   or from the 'righteousness' of 'right relationships'
   that is characteristic of justice,
but they do claim that it is possible to be
   a bearer of the costly faithfulness of God
   in and through the structures and shapes
   of a same-sex relationship,
   expressed through and nurtured by
   acts of sexual intimacy.

Rowan Williams, 'Knowing myself in Christ', Timothy Bradshaw (ed.), *The Way Forward*, Christian Voices on Homosexuality and the Church, Hodder and Stoughton, 1997, p. 18, reproduced by permission of the publishers.

The Bible often gives us clues to help us in the process
of questioning and exploring the ways of God -
as long as we do not expect ready-made answers.

One of those clues is a helpful sentence
in Paul's Letter to the Philippians (1. 9):

'This is my prayer,
that your love may abound more and more,
in knowledge (or perception) and discernment (or wisdom).'

Notice: The process is bathed in prayer.
            The central concern is always 'agape',
                a constant goodwill that stops at nothing to
                secure the well-being of the other.
            Sound decision-making needs knowledge,
                i.e. not prejudice or ignorance.
            Sound decision-making needs discernment,
                i.e. making thoughtful judgments.

Paraphrase and extension in a sexual context:
  Graced by God, we are called to embodied loving,
    in which we enable one another
    to grow in the Spirit of a freedom
    that is neither licence nor impulse,
    but is a responsible recognition and encouragement,
    each of the other,
    towards a mutual maturing and flourishing,
    on a path that demands of us
      the knowledge that is both clear perception
        and accurate touch,
      and the discernment that is both wise pondering
        and prayerful judgment,
    so that we are united with each other,
      and create, each with the other,
    stopping at nothing to secure the ultimate good
      of the other who is beloved.

Explore the basic intentions of the Scriptures,
    each text always in context,
    looking for the centre and heart,
    and the most Jesus-focused direction.

Some will emphasize fidelity to the details of the texts
    and accuse others of self-serving relativism.
Some will emphasize fidelity to the basics
    and accuse others of self-righteous legalism.

I would suggest that these statements are near
    that centre, heart, and focus:

God's unconditional turning towards all people,
    whatever their social contrasts
    based on sex, wealth, and status.
God's acceptance of all people as they are
    and invitation to all people to enter a covenant
whose principal implication is that
    human beings turn to others without condition,
    accept them as they are,
    and invite them to enter that covenant too,
    making it the basis of their relationships
        with one another.
Call it the love that is intimacy in the private sphere,
    and justice in the public sphere,
    and implies kindness, compassion, forgiveness,
    forbearance, discernment, and respect.

NB

1   There is no uniform method of using the Bible
         in the Churches,
      nor within any one Church.

2   The Bible itself shows the struggle to make central
         a Jesus-centred God.

3   Such a God is
      not entirely absent from
         the Hebrew Scriptures,
      often implicit,
      sometimes explicit,

      and not universally present
         in the Christian Covenant,
      often not understood,
      sometimes contradicted.

      The Jewish God and the Christian God
      are not different gods.

2
ENERGETICALLY EMBODYING

'The hum of a generator
  bringing to vibrant life
  material stuff of earth!
How much energy can the human organism stand,
  this organism, that is my flesh-body self?
Ecstasy may be well-nigh intolerable sensation,
  the vibrations becoming so strong and overwhelming
  that pleasure slips over the border into pain.
The hurt may resonate in the very place
  where deep healing is unconsciously sought,
  opening up an ancient wound:
    instead of joy, numbness;
    instead of living flame, dust and ashes.
This place of painful contradiction
  and pleasurable celebration ...

It is a subtle energy,
  the heavenly in the guts of earth,
  the hellish at the very gates of heaven.
Do angels entertain unawares,
  or devils deceive in cloaks of light?
Is God so very close,
  hovering with pulsing wings
  in the vibrations of passionate love?
Is it devilish
  only if there be no laughter and no truth?
Is the place of greatest vulnerability
  the place where we can be most profoundly moved,
  where not only the earth beneath us seems to move,
  but where we know the Love
  that moves the sun and the moon and the stars?'

Source: Jim Cotter, *Pleasure, Pain, and Passion*, Cairns Publications,
2nd edition, 1993, p.87

'Sex is a great hunger,
  a great drive of human energy,
  a late biological development,
  an intense pleasure.

It challenges those divided by it
  to seek and find at a deeper level a unity of being.

It is a gift from God: holy, awesome, explosive.
  Misused, it can blast and wither
  and empty of all significance
  the human beings foolish enough to mistake it.
  Baulked and perverted, it can poison relationships.
Such a gift cannot be ignored or handed back.

It has the features of mystical experience:
  abandon, ecstasy, polarity, dying, rebirth, union.

It has the features of prayer;
  a noticing, a paying attention, a form of address,
  a yearning to communicate more deeply,
  an attempt to reach communion.

It holds out the suggestion of personal fulfilment,
  of union achieved, of community known.

In the past the highest spiritual life was understood
  as implying the renunciation of sexuality.
In the present men and women are asking
  how to live through the fullest experiencing of sexuality
  as their primary road to God.'

Source: Alan Ecclestone, *Yes to God*, Darton, Longman, and Todd, 1975, with acknowledgment.

Sexuality - a wide definition:
'It is our way of being in the world
   as gendered persons,
having male or female biological structures
   and socially internalized self-understandings
   of those meanings to us.
Sexuality means having feelings and attitudes
   about being "body-selves".
It means having affectional orientations
   toward the opposite sex,
   the same sex,
   or quite possibly toward both.
It means having the capacity for sensuousness.
Above all, sexuality is the desire
   for intimacy and communion,
   both emotionally and physically.
It is the physiological and psychological grounding
   of our capacity to love.
At its undistorted best,
   our sexuality is that basic eros of our humanness -
   urging, pulling, luring, driving us
   out of loneliness into communion,
   out of stagnation into creativity.'

Source: James Nelson, *The Intimate Connection: Male Sexuality, Masculine Spirituality*, SPCK, 1992, p. 2, with acknowledgment.

Passion is a good word to use:

a strong emotion almost out of control;

a steady and sometimes stormy anger;

intense erotic love;

enthusiasm for whoever or whatever;

dazzling delight in each other;

an energy that carries you *through* suffering.

So Elizabeth Stuart waves a flag for
  'passionate friendship'
  as the primary way of thinking about
  the practice of and frameworks for our sexuality.

Such a friendship may well be characterized by
  'fierce tenderness'.

Recall that the Hite Report on *Women and Love* in 1987
  found that 87% of married women
  and 95% of single women
  had their deepest emotional relationship
  with a woman friend.

Recall the extraordinary (but need it be so unusual)
  breakthrough into passionate friendship
  between the two heterosexual men,
  Brian Keenan and John McCarthy,
  when they were being held hostage in Beirut.

Sources: Elizabeth Stuart, *Just Good Friends*, Mowbray 1995, with acknowledgment. Mary Hunt, *Fierce Tenderness*, Crossroad, 1991

'I reach into you to reach all mankind;
and the deeper into you I reach
the deeper glows elsewhere the world
and sings of you. It says
to love is the one common miracle.

Feel nothing separate then.
We have translated each other into light
and into love go streaming.'

Source: Brian Patten, *Love Poems*, Unwin, 1984, with acknowledgment.

A sexual-spirited-mystical experience

'I was a Wing Commander in the Royal Air Force. Carl was a Commander in the United States Navy. We had been lovers for two years.' One summer, on leave in the mountains and forests of Turkey, 'we swam ... in a river. Afterwards, as we lay naked in the sunlight, we made love. We had done so many times before, but there was something specially intense about this occasion. Our bodies smelled and tasted of the cool fresh river. We could see a magnificent oak tree, whose leaves danced and rustled. Carl reached his climax inside me. He brought me off with his hand at the same time. We had simultaneous orgasms of explosive force.

At this instant our gaze was drawn to the tree, which had undergone a change. It was ablaze with mysterious life, as if our release of energy had somehow triggered off a reaction in the tree, so that sap raced upwards through it, filling it with power. The best analogy was that a mighty wind was blowing vertically through it and rushing into the blue sky. I thought of the wind of the Holy Spirit which filled the house of the apostles in Jerusalem on the day of Pentecost.

Our sex act had been the expression of our intense love. Love was the force that flowed through the tree and through us. Our bodies were melded. Carl was still inside me. There was a change of consciousness, so that we were at one with each other and with the tree, which seemed to ramify gigantically into outer space. It was a tree of life. The whole landscape - river, forest, mountains, sky - was lit from within. Colours glowed with extraordinary vividness. All was vibrant. Paradise was here and now.

Never had we been so full of life, seemed so beautiful to each other, loved each other so tenderly, been so fused together in body and spirit that each experienced the existence of the other as his own. We saw how everything and everyone was connected in a unity ...

[contd. on next page]

'...Then the vision vanished as suddenly as it had begun. We felt that the mysterious activity was still going on, but that we had lost our awareness of it. It was only now that we realized that during our change in consciousness we had seen no physical motion, heard no sound. For a moment we were dazed at returning to the familiar universe. We discussed what had happened. We had each, independently of the other and yet together, just had an experience that had been virtually identical. Carl said, "The force, whatever it was, obviously didn't mind our being homosexual." We had felt our love (love, not just sex) to be in perfect harmony with the manifestation, indeed to be a part of it. I am a Christian, but I cannot explain it in Christian terms, although I feel it to be in no way incompatible with Christianity. It changed our lives. We could "make connections" as never before. We had more empathy with people. It was one of the reasons why I later retired from the Royal Air Force and became a probation officer.' (Carl died in the following year.) 'I feel that he was part of the *mysterium fascinans* which we once glimpsed together, and that we shall one day be reunited in it...

'I cannot see that God can be kept apart from the sexual act of love, as if it would somehow dishonour him to have any connection with it. It seems to me appropriate to ask for a blessing beforehand, and to offer a heartfelt thanksgiving for love (or even just good sex) afterwards.'

[contd. from previous page]

Source: Peter Cooper, quoted in Peter Sweasey, *From Queer to Eternity*, Cassell, 1997, pp. 88-89, with acknowledgment and personal thanks.

There are two masculine sexual energies,
  the TESTICULAR and the PHALLIC,
and there are two feminine sexual energies,
  the GESTATIVE and the EXERTIVE.

Descriptively,
  the *testicular* is the self-generating and ripening source,
  the stable point of departure,
  characteristically steadfast, resourceful, abiding;
  the *phallic* is the expansive and penetrating energy,
  moving towards a focused goal,
  characteristically targeted, adventurous, goal-oriented;
  the *gestative* receives and allows,
  nurturing towards a point of departure,
  characteristically feeding, receptive, enclosing,
  the *exertive* pushes and births,
  moving from a field of reference,
  characteristically moving with, thrusting, transforming.

When exaggerated,
  the *testicular* is stagnant, festering, sentimental,
  the *phallic* is driving, coercive, argumentative,
  the *gestative* is devouring, stifling, over-protective,
  the *exertive* is rejecting, meddling, premature.

When underused,
  the *testicular* is unstable, testy, impatient,
  the *phallic* is aimless, indecisive, scattered,
  the *gestative* is empty, aloof, impenetrable,
  the *exertive* holds back and is fearful of change.

The masculine energies are manifested
  in a man's outer life and a woman's inner life,
the feminine energies are manifested
  in a woman's inner life and a man's outer life.

[part of a sequence pp. 55-60]

Source: Genia Pauli Haddon, *Body Metaphors*, Crossroad, 1988, with acknowledgment for pages 55-60.

The old understanding was this:

The man initiates,
the woman responds.

God initiates,
Mary responds to bring that initiative to fulfilment.

Biologically,
the entire new being is within the male seed,
the woman is simply the nurturing receptacle.

Theologically,
there can be no better word for God than 'Father',
for Jesus, the intimate 'Abba'.

The new understanding is this:

The man and the woman together
take the initiative,
contributing the four sexual energies
to become intimate,
to create, sustain, and nurture.

Two human beings together reflect
the creative love and power of God.

Biologically,
there is an equal contribution from the man
and the woman.

God's fatherhood and motherhood
are both helpful metaphors
of a supra-personal divine creative source.
To call on God as 'AbbaAmma' is orthodox.

[part of a sequence pp. 55-60]

Source: Genia Pauli Haddon, *Body Metaphors*, Crossroad, 1988

In theology, prayer, and practice,

the phallic is the rising, penetrative, assertive style.

God is enthroned on high,
   King of kings,
   Lord of lords,
   Ruler of the universe,
   almighty, majestic, all-seeing, all-powerful,
   mighty conqueror,
   commander-in-chief of the heavenly host,
   victorious over sin and death,

sending his people forth to conquer new lands,
   wanting us to win the race,
   to fight the good fight,
   to be faithful soldiers.

Climb Jacob's ladder.

Meet God on the mountain top.

Onward Christian soldiers.
The royal banners forward go.

Crusaders.
Salvation Army.
Church Army.

Two-thirds of the pictorial language for God
   in prayers and hymns comes from this style.

[part of a sequence pp. 55-60]

Source: Genia Pauli Haddon, *Body Metaphors*, Crossroad, 1988

In theology, prayer, and practice,

the testicular is the steadfast, conserving style.

God is faithful, unchanging, steadfast,
   the same yesterday, today, and for ever,
   a sure foundation,
   the rock of ages,
   a strong tower.

I will never forsake you.
I am with you always,
   to the end of the ages.

O thou who changest not, abide with me.

Hold to the faith given once and for all,
   consistent through the centuries,
   the long steady tradition.

Faithfully, unfailingly,
   Sunday by Sunday,
   across all the parishes of Christendom,
   the eucharistic action has been done.

[part of a sequence pp. 55-60]

Source: Genia Pauli Haddon, *Body Metaphors*, Crossroad, 1988

In theology, prayer, and practice,

the gestative is the receiving, nurturing style.

God is the suffering servant,
  the loving parent,
  the good shepherd,

the one from whom all blessings flow,
  the bread of life,
  living water for the thirsty,

the one who welcomes the children and the outcast,
  like a mother hen gathering her chicks under her wings,

the compassionate healer,

the comforter,

the shadow of a great rock in the heat of the day,

the one who holds us in the palm of her hand.

Jesus is friend of all,
  the church is a caring community.

We revive circle dancing.

We share the Peace.

[part of a sequence pp. 55-60]

Source: Genia Pauli Haddon, *Body Metaphors*, Crossroad, 1988

In theology, prayer, and practice,

the exertive is the pushing, birthing, transforming style.

God urges us on,
  lays waste and builds up,
  destroys and recreates.

Those whom God loves
  God also chastens.

God is demanding,
  insistent, luring.

We are to give up our lives,
  die with Christ.

It is a fearful thing
  to fall into the hands of the living God.

We experience a dark night of the soul.

God surprises us with a new thing.

God makes all things new.

God is a God of Resurrection.

[part of a sequence pp. 55-60]

Source: Genia Pauli Haddon, *Body Metaphors*, Crossroad, 1988

Overheard outside an underground station,
  one black woman saying to another,
'She's got some good in her:
  you can feel it in your own body.'

High on the National Curriculum
  should be body language
  as well as the English language.

High on the syllabus of religious education
  should be the commandments of love,
  including,
Thou shalt be in touch.
Thou shalt touch.
Thou shalt not commit unloving.

Ask yourself,
  How do I touch others?
  How do I let others touch me?
  What is communicated by handshakes?
  What does touching and being touched mean
    when I focus on different parts of the body?
  What do my friends experience,
    and how do they interpret it,
    and is it the same as mine?
  What kind of physical intimacy is possible
    if, for one reason or another,
    sexual intimacy is not possible?
  What kinds of touch will, here and now,
    encourage intimacy?

And we live in a society that
  is at ease with violent touch
but ill at ease with tender touch -
  especially if it is between men -
  and a second longer than the accepted norm.

'Ay! it's tenderness really ...
Sex is really only touch,
    the closest of all touch.
And it's touch we're afraid of.
We're only half-conscious
    and half-alive.
We've got to come alive
    and aware.
Especially the English
    have got to get into touch
    with one another,
a bit delicate
    and a bit tender.
It's our crying need.'

Source: D.H.Lawrence, *Lady Chatterley's Lover*, with acknowledgment.

'I never told this to anybody before,
  and I really don't know why I'm telling you.
It's just that the last time I saw Rufus,
  before he disappeared,
  we had a fight, he said he was going to kill me.
And, at the very end, when he was finally in bed,
  after he'd cried,
  and after he'd told me so many terrible things -
I looked at him, he was lying on his side,
  his eyes were half open, he was looking at me.
I was taking off my pants ...
  and I was going to stay there,
  I was afraid to leave him alone.
Well, when he looked at me,
  just before he closed his eyes
  and turned on his side away from me,
I had the weirdest feeling he wanted me
  to take him in my arms.
And not for sex, though maybe sex would have happened.
I had the feeling that he wanted someone to hold him ...
  and that, that night, it had to be a man.
I got in the bed and I thought about it
  and I watched his back ...
and I lay on my back and I didn't touch him
  and I didn't sleep ...
I guess I still wonder what would have happened
  if I'd taken him in my arms, if I'd held him,
  if I hadn't been - afraid.
I was afraid that he wouldn't understand that it was -
  only love.
Only love.
But, oh Lord, when he died,
  I thought that maybe I could have saved him
  if I'd just reached out that quarter of an inch
  between us on that bed, and held him ...
And I'll never know, I'll never know.'

Source: James Baldwin, *Another Country*, Michael Joseph, 1963, p. 329, with acknowledgment.

A great teacher of dance,
　　Rudolf Laban was fascinated by the ways
　　in which human beings move,
and he helped his students explore
　　the different dimensions of touch.
His work is drawn upon here
　　because he can help all of us learn
　　something more than the rudimentary ABC of touch:
　　our culture has inhibited our learning of the grammar.
Ask, from the pages that follow,
　　what are the ways in which you touch and are touched,
　　the ways you like and the ways you dislike,
　　the ways you would and would not like.

Concerning *weight*, touch can be
　　strong, firm, gripped, weighty;
　　light, fine, delicate, airborne, buoyant.
Concerning *time*, touch can be
　　sudden, quick, hasty, hurried, momentary;
　　sustained, slow, leisurely, unhurried, prolonged.
Concerning *space*, touch can be
　　direct, straight, undeviating, one way;
　　flexible, wavy, roundabout, many ways.
Concerning *flow*, touch can be
　　bound, controlled, readily stopped;
　　free, fluent, streaming onwards.

(On the following pages,
the first in each set of two examples is of *free* movement,
the second is of *bound* movement.)

[part of a sequence pp. 64-74]

Source: Jean Newlove, *Laban for Actors and Dancers*, Nick Hern Books, 1995, with acknowledgment.

PUNCH is strong, direct, sudden:

> *thrusting:*
>> fork into hay
>> chisel under lid

> *shoving:*
>> shovel into dry sand
>> spade into clay

> *poking:*
>> poker into fire
>> piercing leather

Associated words:

> vigour
> gusto
> spurt
> impact
> lunge
> throb
> jolt
> tough
> shplat

[part of a sequence pp. 64-74]

PRESS is strong, direct, sustained:

> *crushing:*
>> fruit with a crusher
>> granules with a pestle

> *cutting:*
>> leather with a sharp knife
>> wood with a carver's knife

> *squeezing:*
>> squirt washing up liquid
>> squeeze the last bit of toothpaste

Associated words:

> firm
> sturdy
> pulling
> massive
> powerful
> ponderous
> deliberate

[part of a sequence pp. 64-74]

SLASH is strong, flexible, sudden:

>   *beating*
>   a carpet with a beater
>   a nail with a hammer
>
>   *throwing*
>   coal with a shovel
>   a package from hand to hand
>
>   *whipping*
>   egg with a whisk
>   branches of a hedge with a billhook

Associated words:

>   hit
>   swipe
>   throw
>   fling
>   splash
>   sprawl
>   rip

[part of a sequence pp. 64-74]

WRING is strong, flexible, sustained:

> *pulling*
>> a trolley with shafts
>> a cork with a corkscrew

> *plucking*
>> feathers by hand
>> thinning out seedlings by hand

> stretching
>> elastic by hand
>> cloth by hand

Associated words:

> tortuous
> convoluted
> powerful
> twisted
> knotted
> writhe
> screw
> gnarled

[part of a sequence pp. 64-74]

DAB is light, direct, sudden:

>
> *patting*
>> dough
>> levelling index cards
>
> *tapping*
>> keyboard
>> morse key
>
> *shaking*
>> sand in a sieve
>> sprinkling water by hand

Associated words:

> dart
> shoot
> crisp
> pointed
> spritely
> tap
> patter
> bouncy
> staccato
> disjointed
> agitated

[part of a sequence pp. 64-74]

GLIDE is light, direct, sustained:

> *smoothing*
> > cloth by hand
> > lace with an iron
>
> *smearing*
> > whitewash with a brush
> > mortar with a trowel
>
> *smudging*
> > putty with a thumb
> > oil paint with a palette knife

Associated words:

> smooth
> calm
> lullaby
> soothe
> stroke
> pass over
> straight
> legato
> lingering
> glissando

[part of a sequence pp. 64-74]

FLICK is light, flexible, sudden:

> *flipping*
>> a dry towel
>> a wet towel
>
> *flapping*
>> coins when counting them
>> notes when counting them
>
> *jerking*
>> rinsing a bottle
>> snapping string by hand

Associated words:

> flickering
> quivering
> sparkling
> fluttering
> fits and starts
> twitch
> rippling
> frisky

[part of a sequence pp. 64-74]

FLOAT is light, flexible, sustained:

> *strewing*
>> scatter seed by hand
>> scatter powder on a surface

> *stirring*
>> stir water by hand
>> stir oil paint with a stick

> *stroking*
>> a cup to polish it
>> brushing clothes

Associated words:

> gentle
> undulate
> buoyant
> vaporous
> hover
> roundabout
> soft
> caress

[part of a sequence pp. 64-74]

10 March

Sexually,
   you may like to consider the difference between

the power of THRUST,
   strong, direct, sudden,
or: 'Wham, bang, thank you ma'am' ...

the warmth of CARESS,
   light, sustained, flexible,
or: a swiving, rhythmic dance ...

The one may be an exciting thrill,
   but verging on cruelty,
the other may be a calming pleasure,
   but verging on sentimentality.

The one a solo performance,
the other a melting duo ...

And what kind of touch in a tango?

[part of a sequence pp. 64-74]

At the extremes:

strong	cramped
light	sloppy
direct	obstinate
flexible	fussy
sustained	lazy
sudden	hasty
free	flighty
bound	sticky

[part of a sequence pp. 64-74]

To claim that the Word was made flesh
  is to indicate that this was God's pleasure and delight,
  that bodies matter,
  that God is embodied in our flesh-and-blood encounters.

So check this list of words and relate them to Jesus:

laughing   (Mm, yes)

crying   (Of course)

sweating   (Painfully)

urinating   (I suppose so)

defecating   (Yes, but you needn't point it out)

orgasmic   (???)

What do we embrace?

And what does our response to the list
  tell us about ourselves?

At the centre of Jesus's life and work
  were bodies -
    touching,
    eating,
    drinking.
He had a special concern for
  broken bodies,
  untouchable bodies,
  bodies pushed to the edge.
He is portrayed as
  renewed body,
  transfigured body,
  risen body.

(For Elizabeth Stuart,
  resurrection is 'an explosion of re-embodiment'.)

His way of life can be
  embodied among us,
it is within our reach,
it is as close to us as our neighbour.
It can be shared amongst us
  if we really want to,
  if our heart is in it -

and if our hearts are in it,
our bodies will follow.

Dennis Potter said that for him
   religion had always been the wound,
   never the bandage.

If, by reason of your sexuality,
   you have been wounded in the groin by
      clergy,
      Bible,
      dogma,
   whence comes the healing?

From
   masseurs,
   mountain streams,
   poets,

and a few Jesus followers whose
   touch and
   words and
   table
   re-embody his.

Love is proved in absence,
in the heart's longing,
in the impossibility of control,
in living into the ache of being apart,
making of it a kindly space.

For many in our generation,
the religious atmosphere we breathe
is of the absence of God,
the seeming withdrawal of God,
leaving an aching longing.

But the idol has crumbled,
the old supernatural deity is no more,
God as a Separate Very Large Being
has slipped away, has died from our awareness.
The threatening, often cruel,
all-mighty 'Jehovah' god,
over against us, is no more.

In any case, Jehovah was but a name
for the Nameless One,
was but an image against which we are warned.
'I Am That I Am' is always a mystery -
as is the beloved who is different from myself.
It may be that those ancient Hebrew words
are better translated
'I Shall Be There For You In the Unexpected
Encounter Where For You I There Shall Be.'

We discover God now
through the encounter with the other,
through the love grown strong through absence,
and
through the journey within,
learning to live with tenderness towards
that aching longing in the depths of one's being.

God is always becoming embodied,
  taking shape as bodies,
  always being incarnated.
God is always in the midst of our encounters.
God takes her motto from E. M. Forster:
  'Only connect'.
Eckhart called Jesus the 'Great Reminder'
  of this permanent reality.
God ceaselessly works to take
  broken, disconnected, isolated threads
  and weave them into patterns new
    and wondrous strange.
Therefore we are never outside God.
  God is our natural environment
  as much as the sea is to fish.
Therefore the more connected we are
  to one another bodily,
  the more we are enGodded.
So Jesus lived that embodied life,
  constantly touching,
  constantly connecting.
So we are always part of God -
  though God is doubtless a whole
  that is greater than the sum of the parts.
We have to wake up to this reality,
  really see,
  really come alive.

The whole of your life is affected by the ways
  in which you find other people sexually attractive
  and other people find you attractive.

Stunning looks are powerful,
  especially when allied to a beautiful body -
even more when also allied to designer clothes
  in erotic mode.

Not far behind is the rustle of paper
  and the chink of coins,
the power of money.

Looks and wealth *attract*.
  They are *magnetic*.

If you are nondescript in cast-off clothes,
  you possess little,
  you are not much of a *draw*.

But you may *possess* yourself,
  be at ease with yourself,
  and have a *magnetism* of heart and soul,
  and therefore also be a considerable *draw*.
You may thus be more vibrant and sensual
  than the surface beauties.

You may have fewer exciting contacts,
  but deeper and more lasting communion.

And you won't have at the back your mind,
  Will you love me when my looks fade?
  Do you love me only for my bank balance?

To find love in any society,
  look among those who never turn heads
  and just about get by ...

The wealthier you are,
  the more privacy you can guarantee for sexual behaviour
  that you might not wish your relatives
  or your neighbours to know about.
In a large private house with locks on internal doors,
  you have more privacy
  than in a house with six occupants
  and two bedrooms.
In a large limousine with blacked-out windows
  and wide reclining seats
  free from intervening gear lever
  you have more privacy -
  and room -
  than in an ancient draughty mini.
In an exclusive private club
  you have more control over whom you meet
  than in a publicly accessible sauna.
In the great outdoors,
  you have more privacy on your own estate
  than on a public beach or in a public park.

Is it any surprise
  that there is an exchange of power and glamour
  when those with money to burn
  make contact with those with good looks to sell?
And is it any surprise
  that those who break the law
  and are found out
  are usually those towards the bottom
  of the economic pile?
The fewer the resources you have to protect yourself,
  the greater your chances
  of being discovered and disapproved.

A human being may live
  on the surface,
  a small self,
and not
  from the depths,
  a Self in touch with
  THE SELF, the Divine.

The contrast is vital,
  but it is not between
  'flesh' and 'spirit',
  'body' and 'soul',
  but between
  different attitudes and behaviour:

with *illusions*
  or *in truth*;
with *pride and solemnity*
  or with *humility and playfulness*;
by *hanging on*
  or by *letting go*;
by *blocking out* life and others
  or by *letting flow* the life that is in each of us
    and between two of us
    and among all of us;
by being *grace-less*
  or by being *grace-full, gracious*;
by being *split apart (dia-bolic)*
  or by being *joined together (sym-bolic)*;
by being *apathetic*
  or by being *loving*;
by remaining *numb*
  or by becoming *aware*;
by *dis-integration*
  or by *integration.*

Our embodied aim is to become
more physically aware -
  of what is happening,
  of energy and sensation,
  of tone and colour of skin,
  of expression and gesture,
  of posture and movement,
  becoming vibrant, electric, a presence;
more mentally aware -
  with clarity of thought,
  with ease of expression,
  discerning which ideas to value, which to discard;
more *emotionally* aware -
  exploring the range of our feelings,
  accepting their presence,
  allowing them appropriate expression
    in serving the purposes of intimacy and justice;
more *spiritually* aware -
  using imagination and creativity,
  becoming still and silent,
  looking and listening,
  allowing space for the new to take shape.
We can and must work towards an integration
  of these aspects of ourselves,
but the integration itself is a gift,
  and its timing is unpredictable.
When IT happens,
  you know yourself, at least for a moment,
  whole, complete, fulfilled,
  a spirited person, full of energy and character,
  a radiant body, a some-body at last.
You could say that Holy Spirit
  has transformed you into Wholly Spirit,
  or rather Enspirited Body,
  or ...

Play/pray on ...

Homo domesticus
Homo promiscuus
Homo romanticus -
   three ways of horizontal sexuality.

[The 'homo' here is Greek for 'same',
   not Latin for 'man' -
though the second word in each phrase is, I suppose,
   Lat-lish. Sorry.]

Homo transformatus -
   vertical sexuality -
      or making love with God.

The vertical transforms the horizontal,
   bringing a radiant, glowing light to the human body.

When the connection is focused on one person,
   the glow is fulfilling, but temporary and fading.

When the connection is diffused through the whole person
   the whole of the time,
   the glow is permanent and steady.
A moment's intimacy with *that* quality is life-changing,
a person with that quality is always attractive to others,
a finger touch can evoke the shudder of orgasm.

So we are given hints of a glorious dimension to our flesh.
The pleasurable, healing, bonding, and creative aspects
   of sexual relationships are touched
   into something more wonderful still.
There is a deep communication,
   a heavenly, blissful communion,
even when the sexual action is,
   athletically and technically speaking,
   a disaster.

In Lancashire dialect,
  'She's a lovely body'
  does not mean that she *has* a lovely body,
  as if it is an object that she owns,
  but that she is a lovely body,
  she is a beautiful *person*.

I use the word 'body' in that sense,
  the living organism that cannot be split in two
  as 'body' and 'soul',
  but has two dimensions,
  one obvious, the other subtle,
  the one I call 'flesh-body', the other 'soul-body'.

Flesh-body is not to be played down and risen above.
We are not to renounce the sexual
  in order to purify and cool the flesh-body.
Rather do we live our lives as flesh-bodies,
  but when we do so lovingly,
  even if sporadically and not persistently,
  we are feeding the soul-body,
and it is the soul-body that will become
  a total transformation of the flesh-body,
  'clothing it',
  and allowing its present structure
  to fall away and disintegrate.
And sexual energy will make its vital contribution
  to this nourishing of soul-body,
  becoming more and more diffused as energy,
  a hum rather than a crackle.
We shall become surf-riders glowing with light,
  wearing a weight of glory, substantial but light.
St Symeon wrote:
  I participate in the glory,
  and my face shines like my Beloved's,
  and all the parts of my body become bearers of light.
(Yes, *all* the parts ...)

Do men *have* to be
  controllers,
  providers,
  masters,
  directors?
Does biology dictate?

Is the only male bonding allowable
  that of the rugged wilderness trek,
  the army exercise,
to weld men into a fighting unit -
  for warfare on battlefield or in boardroom
  (or in bedroom)?

Does the world of competition
  have to be dog-eats-dog,
  with minimum environmental concern
  and minimum attention to the poor?

Have they never seen a vision
  of relaxation and laughter,
  of flexibility and co-operation,
  even of joy and love?

Source: Jack Nichols, *The Gay Agenda*, Prometheus Books, 1996, with acknowledgment.

Margaret Mead once referred to male friendship in our society as
   'that terrible bang on the back'.

Sister Charles described her sexuality as
   'a pulse that goes right through you.'

Virginia Ramey Mollenkott described her politics as
   'a shiver of solidarity' with other human bodies.

Sources:
Margaret Mead, *Male and Female*, Penguin, 1950,
Sister Charles, quoted in Sally Clines, *Women, Celibacy, and Passion*, André Deutsch, 1993, p. 129
Virginia Ramey Mollenkott, *Sensuous Spirituality: Out from Fundamentalism*, Crossroad, New York, 1993, p. 152, with acknowledgment.

Muscular contractions can be the result of
  paralysis
  body shock
  terror.
They prevent pleasurable sensations
  from spreading through the body.
They perpetuate a fear of letting go of control.
They can be thought to be 'normal',
  as in:
    What's wrong, darling, you moved?
  and:
    Lie back and think of England.
Chronic contraction can be released by
  massage which breaks into tight muscle tissue
  (rolfing is an extreme technique, painful,
  while other methods are gentler).
Parallel to that approach
  is the beating of sado-masochistic sex -
  perhaps another extreme solution,
  of which a variant might be
  the exquisite relating on the very boundaries
  of pain and pleasure.
An everyday example:
  hands after snowballing placed in
  tepid, warm, or hot water,
  and the consequent painful-pleasurable return
    of sensation.
We need to take time to breathe into tensions,
  and to relax into them and through them.
For some to move delicately, carefully, tenderly
  into pleasure
is the experience they are most afraid of.

Those who make so much of the distinction
    between orientation and acts
actually wish to castrate -
    or at least to put sexual desire in a strongbox,
    labelled 'Dangerous',
    'Keep under lock and key'.
Something thought to be infectious and poisonous
    is to be kept in quarantine.

The opposite is not to make every relationship
    genital.
But it is to make every relationship
    sexual -

in the broad sense of bringing to a bonding,
    to any relationship that matters,
the whole of the person,
    including the physical, the emotional,
    the intellectual, the spiritual.

Otherwise, energy is suppressed,
    creativity withers,
    the person fades.

The churches have tried to give sex
  one universal comprehensive meaning.
So they have a struggle to recognize that sex
  may be good in a variety of contexts,
  not least in same-sex relationships,
  and in freely chosen childless marriages.
And they have a struggle to recognize that sex
  in the one approved relationship of marriage
  may well be violent and abusive.

For centuries the churches were obsessed by
  what happens to sperm:
all of it must every time be on course for the egg.
And this is still the case for Roman Catholics,
  for the mutual self-giving must be total,
  and therefore always include the possibility
    of procreation.

What about orgasm without penetration?
  Is it always wrong?
What about a naked cuddle, warm and exciting,
  but without orgasm?
What about a massage that never touches
  'down there' but gives an orgasm?
What about a 'chaste' hug that produces an orgasm?
What about the experience of women
  for whom sexual pleasure is often felt
  throughout the body?
Why should men's experience of local and limited
  sensation be thought the norm - even for them?

Source: Elizabeth Stuart, *Just Good Friends*, Mowbray 1995, with acknowledgment.

3
SERIOUSLY PLAYING

When asked how you came to realize that you were
   lesbian or gay,
you might answer,

That evening when we puréed each other's lips ...

Source: The image comes from Andrew Holleran in his talk 'My Harvard',
published in the Harvard Gay and Lesbian Review, Winter 1994, with
acknowledgment.

Don't make any admissions at all as to your inclinations:
don't masquerade - on any occasion whatsoever -
  in women's clothes,
  take female parts in theatrical performances,
  or use make-up;
don't be too meticulous in the matter of your own clothes
  or affect extremes of colour or cut;
don't wear conspicuous rings, watches, cuff-links,
  or other jewellery;
don't allow your voice or intonation
  to display feminine inflection -
  cultivate a masculine tone and method of expression;
don't stand with your hand on your hip,
  or walk mincingly;
don't become identified with the group of inverts
  which form in every city;
don't let it be noticed that you are bored by female society;
don't persuade yourself into believing that love
  is the same thing as friendship;
don't become involved in marked intimacies with men
  who are not of your own age or set;
don't let your enthusiasm for particular male friends
  make you conspicuous in their eyes,
  or in the eyes of society;
don't occupy yourself with work or pastimes
  which are distinctly feminine;
don't, under any circumstances,
  compromise yourself by word or action with strangers.
Hold frank conversations with suitable persons,
  thereby avoiding mental repression;
encourage every symptom of sexual normalization;
cultivate self-esteem;
become deeply engrossed in a congenial occupation
  or hobby;
observe discretion and practise self-restraint.'

Source: Church of England Moral Welfare Council, 1956: Words fail me ...,
but with acknowledgment.

'Many unthinking heterosexual people
    succumb to the daily bombardment of conditioning
    from the mass media
and live out their lives trapped in oppressive stereotypes.
We should feel compassion for such people,
    not hostility,
for their rejection of all those parts of the self
    that do not conform to the "married-couple" ideal
    is a measure of the loss of contact
    with their own unique sexuality.'

Source: A poster from the 1970s

'Many heterosexual people claim
   that they were just "born that way".
Unfortunately this doesn't hold water.
All human beings are the result of the interaction
   between their substance and their environment,
and heterosexual people, like the rest of us,
   must share in the responsibility for their condition.'

Source: A poster from the 1970s

'If ... young and unrealized homosexuals
   who affect machismo, ultramasculinity,
   and who constitute the hard core
   of our military industrial police Mafia combine
   would go fuck each other
   (and I use that word in its most appreciative
   and loving sense),
   the world would be vastly improved.
They make it with women only to brag about it,
   but are actually far happier in the barracks
   than in boudoirs.
This is, perhaps, the real meaning of
   'Make Love, Not War'.
We may be destroying ourselves
   through the repression of homosexuality.'

So Alan Watts, who also muses that a heaven
   in which one lies 'forever on my Saviour's breast'
   could be fun for nuns,
but for a heterosexual man is an invitation to boredom
   in a homosexual paradise.
'This is not to say that I condemn homosexuality,
   but only that I do not enjoy it.'

Source: Alan Watts, *In My Own Way*, Vintage Books, 1973, p. 42, quoted in Jack Nichols, *The Gay Agenda*, Prometheus Books, 1996, with acknowledgment.

Pornographic	Erotic
parts	whole
mechanical	personal
one-dimensional	multi-dimensional
separating	connecting
use *of* the other	enjoyment *with* the other
hatred of the flesh	love of the flesh
violating	enhancing
boring	interesting
repetition	variety
grunts and clichés	range of sounds and words

NB The contrast is not between the presence and absence of pictures and descriptions of sexual intercourse.

Making Eucharist and Making Love:
  the parallels:

Greeting

Willingness to be open and truthful to the other

Conversation between us, sharing of our stories

Unfolding of new meanings of our love

Affirmation of the other

Awareness of and concern for others

Confession and forgiveness

The touch of healing and peace

A naked offering, a gift of oneself to the other

Rejoicing, gratitude, pleasure

A loss of control and breaking of boundaries

Mutual giving and receiving of life

Being impelled beyond this encounter to love the world

Parallels are often interesting.
What do you talk about,
  what do you keep quiet about?

'Your decision as to whom and how much to tell
  probably depends on how friendly you are
    with a particular person,
  but complete secrecy can be a tremendous burden.'

That is a quotation from a pamphlet published by
  Abbot Laboratories, *Living with your Ileostomy*.
It is about how to cope with wearing a plastic bag
  to take waste products from your body.

I didn't want to look at the pamphlet.
I felt embarrassed - and a little bit repelled.
But I can easily understand
  how you could feel it a stigma if you had to wear one.
People might withdraw and keep their distance
  if they knew the truth.

The pamphlet tries to reassure the - er -
  is it 'sufferer' or should it be 'wearer'?
There are many of you around - even athletes,
  you can lead an ordinary life,
    there is nothing to be ashamed of.

It sounds as if it's copied from a pamphlet
  for a newly aware gay or lesbian teenager.
I particularly like 'even athletes'.

The military mind believes it is difficult to run an army
  if the general is in love with the captain,
  let alone the sergeant or the private.

It is an argument that has been used
  to exclude women from the forces,
and is still used
  to exclude those of homosexual orientation
  and to exclude any close relationships
    between those of different rank.

A point or two:

1 Regulations for training people for emergencies
      and for the use of force
   are hardly appropriate for ordinary life
     where laws discourage force.

2 Such regulations need not exclude relationships
      between soldier and civilian.
   (In any case, marriages so occur.)

3 If men were free to love men,
     even to hug each other anywhere,
   (well, perhaps not when other lives are at risk),
     and not only on station platforms,
  there would be no need for war.

4 That the law, especially the military law,
     is concerned so much about sex between men,
   (and the male mind has such little imagination
  that it never thinks that women may have devised
  variations of sexual pleasure among themselves),
     shows that it is more concerned
     with the distribution of power
     than with the distribution of love.

Old comparison:

> Sex is like killing:
> on the whole don't,
> but there are a few exceptions.

New comparison:

> Sex is like eating:
> on the whole do,
> but be prudent, careful, responsible.

Some parallels:

> Hatred of the flesh -
>   self-starvation and
>   sexual desire repressed or suppressed;
> and the other side of the same coin -
>   gluttony and
>   indiscriminate sex.
> In either there is no love of the flesh.

> Self-abuse -
>   diet of coke and chips and
>   disgust with anything sexual;
> and the contrast -
>   careful healthy diet and
>   the self-love of 'your friendly hand'
>   (a Gaelic euphemism).

Rhythms:
    fasting and feasting;
    restraint and celebration;
    wholesome everyday food
        and a candlelit supper for two;
    both food and sex can be carriers of
        holy communion.

If sex is compared with hospitality,
   we recognize that there are boundaries,
and that both acts flourish
   where there is
      trust,
      intimacy,
      communion,
      healing,
      celebration.
Our horror at the murder of Duncan
   while he imagines himself an honoured guest of Macbeth
and our horror at the sexual abuse of children
   stem from the pain, chaos, and damage
   caused in human life
   when a sacred trust is betrayed.

It is thought that the Church of England
   has never made much impression on the French
   because English people have found eating snails
   to be a disgusting, stomach-churning, unnatural habit,
   and so have offended French hospitality.
The French have been heard to insist
   that to refuse hospitality is most unnatural ...

If you are a 'masculine male'
    are happily married with three or four children,
    and find your sexual life satisfying,
then anything *other* is bound to seem to you
    to be *less* than what you have.
And what *seems* to you to be a handicap
    comes to be *defined* as such.
That definition includes
    less than whole,
    lacking in something essential,
    not having true validity.
The person so defined
    may decide to play along,
    or may simply assume that there is nothing more
    to be said or done.
After all, there is a long tradition of such separations:
    conformist and nonconformist,
    king (powerful) and jester (weak 'fool'),
    healthy and crippled,
    the rich man in his castle
        and the poor man at his gate.
If you are willing to be 'minstrel-ized',
    the rewards can be considerable:
    you are warm, fed, and sheltered,
    and may be a trusted presence at the king's high table.
Clowns and nonconformists are always necessary
    for laughter and entertainment,
and in a world of separations,
    to be prophetic and warn.
After all, the fool is the only one trusted and allowed
    to tell the king the truth:
    he has no stake in the power games at court.
But can the powerful admit that, it is only from the fools
    that they can learn what it means to be wise?
Even well meaning but patronizing pity
    can be deftly turned by the response:
Maybe not as fertile, but often just as fruitful.

A number of rams were separated from the ewes
  for some weeks.
When let loose, some of them ignored the ewes
  and were interested only in one another.

In flocks of Canada geese,
  some of the males in the flock were observed
  to be not interested in the females,
but they had the important social role
  of patrolling the boundaries of their territory,
so as to be able to warn the busy breeders
  of any approaching danger.

They are the watchmen and lookouts -
  in human terms
    the prophets,
    the artists,
    the 'berdaches':
  those with whom the majority are often ill at ease,
  those whom the mature among that majority appreciate.

The 'berdache' of traditional native American society:

The boundary person

needed by a mature society;

needing that society to prevent isolation,
    whether social isolation
    or its reflection in isolated and isolating sex;

often ambivalent in gender,

typically
    a teacher,
        guiding people over the boundary
        between childhood and adulthood,
    a healer,
        familiar with the boundaries of
        sickness and health,
    a shaman,
        familiar with the boundaries of
        life and death.

Such a role
    is broadly sexual,
    is inclusive of sexuality,
    needs an awareness of sexual energy,
        and its use in a non-genital way:

the young person growing up is helped
    to become sexually aware and responsible;
the sick person is helped
    to be in touch with the body's healing energies;
the dying person is helped
    to approach death
    as the supreme occasion of union and creativity.

The 'berdache' is
  the mediator,
  the go-between,
  the inventive and creative person,
  the 'seer' with double vision,
  the explorer of the unknown.

The tribe recognized the young berdache
  through listening to the growing child's dreams.
The response was to cherish someone who is not typical,
  not to try and change that person,
  nor to stigmatize and shun.
Here is someone to be treated as mysterious and holy,
  as exceptional, not as deviant.
The spirits must have taken more than usual care
  in creating this person.
The Great Mystery has something to teach us
  through this special person.

The Navajo have the word 'nadle'
  to describe such 'a changing one',
  'one who is transformed'.

In their creation myth, a nadle, Turquoise Boy,
  saves his people from a great flood
  by finding a large hollow reed
  up which they all climbed into the present world.

The survival of humanity depends
  on the inventiveness of the nadle.

Source: W. L. Williams, *The Spirit and the Flesh: Sexual Diversity in American Indian Culture*, Beacon Press, Boston, 1986, with acknowledgment.

A television advertisement of the late nineties:

She drops her shopping outside the supermarket.

He squats down and helps her gather the scattered goods.

Their eyes meet and sparkle.

A second man appears and whisks the first away.

The first looks back over his shoulders and shrugs them.

She smiles ruefully.

Give the thumbs up
  when you emerge from under their thumb.

Beware of thumbing a lift
  in somebody else's vehicle:
you may be taken where you do not want to go,
  and the road less travelled
  may be the one you need to take.

Be a sore thumb
  that tells the whole body
  that something is wrong.
Visible and unprotected,
  it makes others wince.

What kind of beauty captivates you?

'Colour me beautiful'?

The body beautiful,
   finely sculpted and honed
   from hours in the gym?

Or skin deep?

What about the beauty
   that is within,
   that is waiting to be expressed,
   that comes to light through the eyes,
   that transforms a face for an eternal moment?

For most of us,
   one look in the mirror is enough to make us glad
   that beauty is in the eye of the beholder ...

And men are *so* oppressed:
   some of them may come to think of themselves
   as handsome,
   but *beautiful*?

A nomad depends upon settlers
   for hospitality on a journey.
Travelling through Ireland,
   with its long history of hospitality to strangers,
the welcome was nearly always warm,
   but it was only the writer's gay hosts
   in Belfast and Dublin,
   who had panache and flair.
On the towels of Belfast
   was a decorative parasol
   such as would usually deck a cocktail.
On the occasional table of Dublin
   were profiteroles and spring water.
I recall E. M. Forster writing of an aristocracy
   of the 'sensitive, the considerate, and the plucky ...
   there is a secret understanding between them
   when they meet ...'

Heaven may not be a bad place
  for lesbian and gay people:

There will, we are told, be no marrying
  or giving in marriage.

Those on the margins will be drawn into the centre.

There will be great style in the celebrations,
  with plenty of opportunity for high camp.

The casting down of golden crowns around the glassy sea
  looks like a gesture of defiance and flair,
  with a perhaps unredeemed desire to be noticed.

The heavenly banquet will probably be organized
  by those used to Gay Pride parades.

It will all be a great contrast to present suffering.

Justice and friendship will be characteristic of its
  political and social life:
it will be a city,
  though one hopes not one without gardens.

Sly cheap mockery?
A misuse of the Bible?
Playing with our ancestors?
Having fun with ancient images?

What clothes do you wear in church?

Who is very colourful -
  because they like to dress that way,
  because they like to stand out in a crowd,
  because they think it's a party,
  because it goes with the job?

What is
  fashion,
  costume,
  badge,
  uniform?

What do you judge to be
  modest,
  acceptable at Easter,
  flamboyant,
  flaunting?

Who makes it obvious who they are? Think of
  Salvation Army officers,
  clowns,
  dog collars,
  military police,
  academics,
  choir members,
  cross-dressers,
  etc.

The unexpected, the unusual, the seemingly out of place -
  these always disturb us.
Are they the necessary boundary crossers,
  the disturbers of our false peace?

Bishop: No, young man, these are *robes*:
  they are not *drag*.

A gay man troubled by his sexuality
  wandered for hours through the streets
  of the east end of London.
He went into a Wimpy Bar
  and suddenly and unexpectedly
  imagined that Jesus was sitting opposite him
  and saying,
You are all right as you are.
It was a life-changing moment.

Some time later he told this story in Canada.

The Canadian equivalent of the put-down 'poofter'
  is 'wimpy'.

And the nearest Canadian equivalent to a 'Wimpy Bar'
  is a 'Dairy Queen'.

Extracted from an interview with a celebrity
in a newspaper column:

How often do you have sex?
On special occasions.

What single thing would improve your quality of life?
More special occasions.

'If you survey a map of the British Isles,
   it looks as though the English had settled comfortably
   into the gentler terrain
   and pushed those races whom they considered
   as their inferiors
   into rocky, chilly areas of the available land mass.
Both Wales and Scotland are
   conspicuously lumpy territory,
   hardly arable and deeply hostile to human habitation.
I think what also sticks in the gut
   of both the Welsh and the Scots
   is the history of betrayal by the English,
who in spite of their self-congratulatory view of themselves
   have perpetrated centuries of dirty tricks on nations
   which they consider less than themselves ...
(A)s I stepped from the plane (at Glasgow) I said,
   "I did not mean that unpleasantness at Glencoe.
   I can't think what came over me."
I was greeted warmly ...
The "gay" movement appeals to Scotland -
   maybe it's kinship with the underdog.
The idea of freedom from oppression is dear to the Scots
   and they have always believed in faeries.
As that notable Scot Mr J. M. Barrie explained in *Peter Pan*:
   "The white ones are the little boys
   and the mauve ones are the little girls,
   and then there are the blue ones
   who are all the little sillies
      who don't know what they are."
No one in Scotland seemed to mind such subversive talk.
Mr Barrie became the richest playwright of his day.'

Source: Quentin Crisp, *The Guardian*, NB It was pointed out by a reader that Glencoe was a battle of the clans, but far be it from me to query Quentin Crisp! 1996, with acknowledgment.

An American comedian pointed out
  that the Bible contains six homosexual admonitions,
  and over three hundred heterosexual admonitions.

Does this demonstrate that heterosexual people,
  while not necessarily more immoral
  than homosexual people,
  nevertheless need more supervision?

...!

Almost all gay men
  have been naked in bed with a woman.

(They were very very young at the time,
  and have no memory of an experience
  which doesn't seem to have influenced
  their adult sexuality in a heterosexual direction.)

A vicar somewhat absentmindedly misread
   the old introduction to the marriage service
   in the Book of Common Prayer.

'If any man can show any just cause
   why these two persons may not
   joyfully be loined together,
   let him now speak,
   or else hereafter for ever hold his peace.'

It is rumoured that certain reformers
   wished to make this change permanent,
   since it reflected a more positive attitude to sex
   than the Church had previously given,
but the lawyers, as always, thought otherwise.

During the debates in the British Parliament in July 1998
    on the proposal to lower the age of consent
    for homosexual acts from 18 to 16,

in the House of Commons
    the average age of those
    who spoke *for* the motion
    was 44,
    with only one speaker over the age of 60;

in the House of Lords
    the average age of those
    who spoke against the motion
    was 74,
    with only one speaker under the age of 60.

Not that this statistic proves anything:
    it could be used to suggest the wisdom of the elders;
    or to suggest the Commons was more in touch
        with the will of the people;
    or to show that such figures merely reflect
        the difference in average age of the members
        of the two houses.

4
BECOMING VISIBLE

Strategies of survival:

1 The most significant part of your life
   and the energy you put into it
   is hidden from the wider community.

2 The hidden life develops its own codes
   and often its own secret language.

3 There is a heightened sense of humour
   which is used
      a) to lighten the burden
      b) to outsmart the opposition.
   Among gay men it becomes 'camp':
   humour, flamboyance, irony, style.

4 There is an unspoken collusion with the majority,
   who may be tolerant
   as long as nothing is visible
   and they don't have to react publicly.

5 The group is highly vulnerable
   to being scapegoated
   and placed in ghettoes, if not worse.

6 When able to be occasionally visible,
   the means chosen is often that of carnival,
   with colour, music, and flair:
      fairgrounds;
      Notting Hill Carnival;
      Gay Pride March and Festival.

As a bulb,
   you need to discover the soil in which you can grow.
And you can grow so far in the dark,
   behind the closet door.
To flower you have to come into the light of day,
   and be seen.

Are you really safe,
  let alone free,
if you live in secrecy,
  afraid of being discovered?
And even if you get used to it,
  is this a healthy way to live?
Are you not dividing yourself in two?
Is it not self-oppressive
  to collude with such a demand
  from those who cannot cope
  with your being visible?
Is it not self-hating
  to pretend to be what you are not,
  to live in silent deceit and hypocrisy?
Are you not belittling yourself,
  adding to your anxieties,
  de-pressing your energy?
And are you not denying others
  the unique gifts you have to offer?

If you surrender to intolerance,
  you allow it to grow,
  you encourage society to stigmatize,
  you feed homophobia,
  you make discrimination more likely.

If you take the expedient path,
  institutions will find it expedient
  to ignore, suppress, and silence you.

... Does my sassiness upset you?
Why are you beset with gloom?
'Cause I walk like I've got oil wells
Pumping in my living room...

... Does my haughtiness offend you?
Don't you take it awful hard
'Cause I laugh like I've got gold mines
Diggin' in my own back yard...

... Does my sexiness upset you?
Does it come as a surprise
That I dance like I've got diamonds
At the meeting of my thighs?...

Source: Maya Angelou, *And Still I Rise*, Virago, 1986, pp. 41-42, ©1978 by
Maya Angelou. Reprinted by permission of Random House, Inc.

Bisexual people
  make others feel very uncomfortable
  because, like those who are trans-gender,
  they undermine distinct categories with clear boundaries.
Gay and lesbian people react:
  You can have all the benefits of being heterosexual
  and you can hide your same-sex relationship
  when it is politic.
Heterosexual people react:
  You are at best eccentric and at worst degenerate.
The churches react:
  You can't possibly be faithful.

It is at least possible that most of us are capable of both,
  but that the majority are socialized
    into being thoroughly heterosexual
 (and to choose a mate from our own class, colour, creed)
  and the minority who are not
    are thought to be completely homosexual.
Lesbian women and bisexual people are conscious
  of the fluidity of our human sexuality,
that it does not seem to be that biology is destiny;
that social forces shape us significantly;
and also that we can sometimes *choose*.

That sounds dangerous and subversive to those in control.
So also:
  spies who are at ease in 'another country';
  artists who explore the future and disturb the present;
  carers who insist on valuing those thought 'expendable';
  priestly figures who are at home in a different reality.
Transvestites, bull dykes, and drag queens also disturb -
  and the latter were in the forefront
    of the gay liberation movement
  when it began outside the Stonewall Inn in New York
    in 1969.

Source: Elizabeth Stuart, *Just Good Friends*, Mowbray 1995, with acknowledgment.

Post AIDS
it may be risky to be visible,
it is dangerous to be invisible.

What has become visible is people
where previously what was visible was only sex
(and that occasionally and often scandalously).

What has become visible and admirable
is what was previously admirable but hidden -
the widespread characteristics of gay men:

'male tenderness,
being at ease with the body,
sensitivity to vulnerability,
realism about sexuality,
deep acceptance of other people's weaknesses,
refusal to dismiss anyone as "unclean",
artistic flair and creativity,
intuitive grasp on how to engage society's imagination,
sense of irony,
genius for celebration,
ability to move from gentle humour
to well-crafted anger,'

and a taking back from the world of medicine
the process of dying
and from the world of church and commerce
the rituals of death.

Source: Michael Vasey, *Strangers and Friends*, Hodder & Stoughton, 1995, p. 239, reproduced by permission of the publisher.

The phrase 'the gay community' is used too loosely.

It hides the fact of a bewildering variety of lifestyles
   among lesbian and gay people.

It hides the fact that very few - if any - neighbourhoods
   are exclusively gay,
   even if they are often self-designated as 'villages',
   and the word 'ghetto' is less to do with geography
   than with symbols and mindsets.

It hides the fact that the subculture is 'episodic':
   it surfaces and submerges with
   the temporary popularity of certain pubs and clubs,
   the success or failure of annual events,
   the limited timespan of particular campaigns,
   the changing desires of particular people
      from identifying with the 'scene'
      to heading for the quieter waters of domesticity.

Socially, the 'scene' is a reality,
   a strategy for lesbian and gay people
   to engage with those parts of their lives in an open way
   that is impossible elsewhere.
Politically, 'constituency' is a more accurate word
   than 'community'.

It is now almost a cliché,
   that I don't mind what they do
   as long as it isn't in the street
   frightening the horses.
It is not illegal (neither fully lawful)
   to participate in a homosexual act
   in private,
   which means that the rest of the world
   has to be locked out.
Sexuality is privatized
   into the realm of home and family:
even weddings can now take place
   in places of personal choice
   rather than churches or registries
   designated by the community.
Churches themselves become semi-privatized.
   The language of the 'church family'
   demonstrates that they are perceived and used
   in a way similar to our homes -
   as places of refuge from the public world.
It is very difficult to have good public discourse
   about matters of sexuality.
And it is no wonder that gay pride marches
   are so disturbing.
Sex is clearly of public concern
   in a society where procreation is its only purpose.
The availability of contraception is another factor
   that makes most people think sex is a private matter.
We need to discover something deeper:
   that sexual energy,
   that the human desire to unite and create,
is all-pervasive:
   it may be suppressed,
   but potentially it is there to infuse
   all our activities, public and private,
   with warmth and connection,
   with justice and new ways of living as communities.

This is Section 28 of the Local Government Act of 1988:
    A local authority shall not
    a) intentionally promote homosexuality
        or publish material with the intention
        of promoting homsexuality:
    b) promote the teaching in any maintained school
        of the acceptability of homosexuality
        as a pretended family relationship.

One *possible* interpretation of 'promote' is that
    anything you say must be discouraging.
One *certain* interpretation is that
    you must not be even-handed,
    putting before young people
    both hostile *and* friendly opinions.
This means that a teacher cannot educate,
    only indoctrinate.

To call a relationship 'pretend'
    is to imply that it is built on a lie,
and does not allow any other interpretation:
    e.g. a 'different' kind of family.
It also ignores the fact that many lesbian and gay couples
    would not describe themselves as a family
    unless they had the care of children.

In practice, the Act does not get dramatized in the courts,
    but largely hidden in silent censorship,
    what is *not* said, *not* discussed, *not* made available,
    in declining to invite a lesbian poet to a public meeting,
    in removing magazines from libraries
    in dismissing teachers from their posts.

Coming out redeems:
    it saves you from the inner suicide of the closet
    (which at heart is a place of isolated darkness);
    it saves you from your destructive refusal
    of the divine *gift* of your sexuality.

Coming out empowers:
    it releases bound up energy,
    the anger and passion you have denied;
    it enables you to contribute to the well-being
    of others who are lesbian and gay.

Coming out reconciles:
    it reconciles you to yourself,
    for you no longer have to live a lie,
    splitting yourself in two;
    it reconciles you to others,
    because truth-telling always brings you closer
    to those who really matter.

To be closeted is to be
    deadened,
    divided,
    dis-graced.

To be out in the open is to be
    enlivened,
    made more whole,
    full-of-grace.

Affirmations:

The deep desire to be united to another of your own gender
    in an intimate loving relationship
    is a *good* desire.

More and more people in our society
    know at least a few lesbian and gay couples -
    in their families, among their friends,
    at their places of work, in their churches -
    whose lives are every bit as sacrificial and fruitful
    as those of married couples.

More and more people are saying,
    What's the fuss?

'Your silence will not protect you.'

If you remain silent about being lesbian or gay,
if you do not acknowledge your partner in public,
if you habitually 'pass for straight' in social settings,
   you will experience in varying degrees
      feeling left out,
      feeling invisible,
      feeling isolated,
      embodying stress,
      living a lie
        (certainly a white one,
        probably a dark grey one),
      living below your potential.

It is a sin of omission
   to draw limits on the work
   towards maturity and fullness of being
   to which all human beings are called.

We cannot resolve conflicts
   until we take courage to tell our stories,
   until we face the fear of rejection.

And we need safe spaces to become more at ease
   in trying out the telling of those stories.

Any chance of churches becoming such safe spaces?

Source of quote at top of page: Audré Lorde, African American lesbian poet.
Source for page: Melanie A. May, 'Breaking Down the Dividing Wall', *The Ecumenical Review*, vol. 50, no. 1, January 1998, pp. 41ff, with acknowledgment.

Life can be elegant in closets.
   They can be beautifully furnished,
   and most of the time you can forget about
   the locked doors and shaded windows.
You can find elegance and truth in mathematics,
   but bodily you can be living an awkward lie:
   you may have as little idea of its language
   as most of us do about mathematics.
You can find protection in a charmed circle,
   who will protect your secret by closing ranks,
   but woe betide you if you are 'found out'.
   You will then be shunned, excluded, isolated.
To be 'found out' or to be 'outed'
   is not to choose the moment or the audience.
To 'come out' is to take responsibility
   for a closed secret becoming an open secret.
To remain isolated
   is to lose the identity that comes
      from making inner connections
      and from belonging to a community,
   is at best to conform in public
      and yearn in private,
   is to be aware of faint echoes of a language
      you never take an opportunity to speak,
   is to keep yourself away from all possibility of love,
   is to be on the road to suicide.
Even a closet for two
   can become a gruesome twosome,
   a relationship that can turn in on itself
   because it is not stimulated and challenged
   by interaction with others.
Is it not better to be hated for what you are
   than loved for what you are not?
It is only when enough people 'come out',
   especially couples in mature relationships,
   that the *public* imagination will shift,
   and others *see* what is good through the words they *hear*.

If you have been betrayed,
    or let down, or not recognized,
you may well turn to betrayal in revenge,
    and become a spy.
If you have learned how to dissemble,
    how to have two different identities
    in different social circumstances,
you grow up with one very good qualification
    for the secret services.
So the connection between male homosexuality
    and treachery has some foundation.
It is a myth,
    a small truth blown up out of all proportion -
    after all there are thousands times more gay people
    in this country than there are spies -
    but myths are emotionally very powerful.
If you think that it is your duty to marry
    and raise children,
those who think that this is a matter of choice,
    and refuse to put their energy into happy families,
are bound to be suspected of heresy
    against the social and possibly religious norms.
If you say that you would prefer
    not to have been born homosexual in inclination,
    and that you wish you could be heterosexual
    so that you could marry and have a family,
you will perhaps be pitied
    and given an honorary role in an extended family.
If you say that you are quite contented to be homosexual,
    and that you are not at all repelled by women,
    and that you could -
    if your life or a hundred thousand pounds were at stake -
    engage in heterosexual intercourse,
    but you choose not to,
and if the majority of the population disagrees with you,
    you are not likely to be often found
    at the tables of the respectable and influential.

We are called to
   '... take upon's the mystery of things,
   As if we were God's spies.'   [*King Lear*, V. iii. 16-17]
To be an 'espier'
   is to see more clearly than most,
   to be as hawks
   or as riders of the range,
   to be 'frontier scouts',
   ahead of the pioneering wagon train,
   scanning new territory,
   'the other country'.
Espiers are sustained
   only by hidden, unspoken marks of recognition:
   only in one another do they find a 'home'.
Hearth and home, kith and kin,
   never come first:
   they are at best temporary resting places.
The call to journey on may come at any time,
   even in the middle of the night.
Their God is revealed always as Future,
   beckoning on and away from idols of security,
   calling some to live always on frontiers,
   scouting the future landscape
   for others more timid to follow and settle.

Come out into the light of day,
   out of the closets of fear.
Do not betray either companions -
   or foes -
   (for they need your truths too)
   by cowardly or over-prudent silence.
There is much more freedom yet to be claimed,
   and freedom is never easily won.
Of course there is risk:
   you cannot escape the conditions of your time.
And of course your freedom is never without limits,
   not least because you have to respect others' boundaries,
but there is usually more territory to inhabit
   than you have been led to believe.
Press the limits outwards.
Keep pressing your presence
   gently, insistently, persistently, boringly.
Keep claiming steadily that it is not an offence
   to be open to the street,
   to the public world,
with your identity and your history,
   and your claim that the world would be a better place
   if you were heeded.
You don't have to *approve* of everything others do,
   or *approve* of everything that you yourself do.
   You don't have to *approve* of every title in a bookshop.
But do not let others use that argument against you,
   as if you have to be perfect before being accepted.
If you try and pretend that you are,
   you fall into the same hypocritical trap
   that spoils the lives of all self-righteous moralists.

Do most human beings still live out their days
   in quiet desperation?
Do too many still wander around in a grey miasma
   of their own unrecognized intrigue?
Do we play games by rules so ancient
   that we simply absorbed them rather than learnt them -
   forgetting that rules can always be changed?
Do we agree with Steve Biko,
   the black leader in South Africa who died in prison,
   that nothing helps the oppressor
   so much as the mind of the oppressed?

The contrast is with the joy and relief of saying
   No more.
From this day on,
   at the very least I will be honest with *myself*.
My eyes and ears have been opened.
The lion in me is at last flexing those throat muscles.
Energy begins to move.
Paralysis loosens its grip.
Defensive armour begins to drop away.
The fog clears.
It hurts, yes, by God it hurts -
   and that's not swearing, it's true.
Layer after layer of accumulated pain
   comes to the surface to be dispersed.
A choice has been made,
   not to be safe and cocooned and numb and dead,
   but to risk and be vulnerable and to feel and to be alive.

When you emerge from the closet

and dismantle the cubicle,

you begin to move beyond cupboard love.

Where are you at ease as your sexual self?

In churches?
In monasteries?
In a suburban semi?

(The answer to all three *may* be Yes ...)

In closet or apart-ment?
  (Only in secret.)

In cottage, sauna, dunes?
  (In semi-public spaces, yet private.)

In a fortress-like home?
  (Privately, but not secretly.)

In a terraced house?
  (As near like the neighbours as you can get)

In a corner house with a verandah?
  (Open to the street, part of the 'village'.)

The much appreciated spiritual writer Henri Nouwen
  began to come to terms with his sexuality
  only towards the end of his life.
As an ordained Roman Catholic,
  shaped and weighed down by the expectations
  of church and society,
  internalized in his own persona,
he faced an unresolvable dilemma,
  stuck between three possible courses of action:

To stay celibate and ordained
  and come out as gay.
To leave the ordained ministry
  and be open to a sexual relationship.
To remain publicly what he had always been,
  and privately to be open to a sexual relationship.

To choose the third would have been
  a betrayal of his integrity.
To choose the second would have been
  a betrayal of his vocation.
To choose the first would have been - or so he thought -
  to become identified with a single issue.

He chose none of these,
  and he remained celibate, ordained, and closeted.

He said to a friend,
  'If I came out I would be labelled
  as just another gay priest writing from my sexuality
  and not my spirituality.'

Might he not have been appreciated even more -
  as a very special gay priest,
  whose writing gained even more spiritual depth
  because it had embraced his sexuality?

Source: Michael Ford, *Wounded Prophet*, Darton, Longman, and Todd, 1999, with acknowledgment.

A book about Henri Nouwen is entitled *Wounded Prophet*.
  Is it unfair to say that he might have nursed his wounds,
  receiving palliative treatments
  for an incurable condition,
  never thinking there might be a cure,
  living in an organization that ran superb clinics
  but never thought of giving up the weapons
  that caused the wounds in the first place?

He himself endured the anguish of a breakdown.
  Intellectually he knew the direction he should move in
  and he talked and wrote publicly
  about being embodied,
  (he had always been an embodied public *performer*.)
  Practically, he neglected his bodily well-being,
  and he died prematurely of a heart attack ...

It may be possible in other churches
  to choose to live both as an ordained minister
  and as openly gay but not celibate,

but most who do so
  either keep fairly quiet about their partners,
  or exercise a ministry on the margins of the institution,

and in the present climate,
  at least in the Church of England,
are either closing the closet door shut with a bang,
  or leaving the ordained ministry altogether.

The window of survival is narrow enough,
  the light in which to flourish
  sometimes seems to be growing,
  and sometimes seem to be on the verge
  of being extinguished.

Source: Michael Ford, *Wounded Prophet*, Darton, Longman, and Todd, 1999, with acknowledgment.

To leave

  home
  church
  'god'

is to enter a wilderness
or to go into exile.

If exile,
you may hope to return,
  but you will be marked for ever by that exile;
you may hope for restoration,
  but the old will have a new dimension.
Home will be different now.
For the people of Israel,
  exile challenged them to stretch their belief
  from a God who favours us more than anyone else
  to a God who is God for everyone.

If wilderness,
you cannot hope to return,
 and you will be marked for ever by that wilderness;
you may hope for something new,
  but you will take with you much of the old,
  more than you may realize at the time.
A new vision of God awaits you in the wilderness,
  and a new way of life in the promised land.
Meanwhile,
  oases will have to serve
  as temporary celebrations of what is to come.

Restoration or renewal?
Novelty or new unfolding?
A place for both reformist and for revolutionary?

5
COUNTERING REACTIONS

Two emotive words are often used
  in conversations about unfamiliar sexual acts:

unnatural
disgusting

They are used
  in an attempt to clinch arguments
  or as an offhand and sometimes angry dismissal.

If you can reassure yourself that something you dislike
  is unnatural and/or disgusting,
then you can condemn it as wrong.

It will be punished

  by law:
    fines,
    imprisonment,
    exile,
    death;

  by ostracism:
    neighbours
      put excrement through letter boxes,
      write hateful anonymous letters,
      throw bricks through windows,
      set houses on fire,
      anything to get a person to move;

  by God:
    hellfire;

  by God's earthly representatives:
    excommunication.

Such attitudes and actions are made respectable

by doctors

  describing damage to rectal tissue;

    (assuming that all homosexual acts are
      violent anal penetration:
    tell that to
      lesbians,
      gay men who never have anal sex,
      gay men who find it 'natural'
        to be gentle and careful
        before riding the waves of passion.)

by police

  describing an offence caused by sex in public;

    (assuming that this gives the go-ahead
    to flush out by searchlight those
    who are otherwise invisible in bushes at night:

    this fails to make the distinction between
    private behaviour visible to the public
    and private behaviour in public places,
    but invisible unless deliberately sought out,
    e.g. steamed up car in quiet lane at 2 a.m.)

[contd. on next page]

by theologians

who talk of same-sex attraction and action
as 'an intrinsic moral disorder',
desires that *by their very nature*
are 'all over the place',
'out of place',
hence 'unnatural';

who talk of same-sex actions as sins,
and sometimes even regard the attraction itself
  as sinful.

If 'sin' is corporate and personal life
whenever and wherever it tends
  towards the dreadful 'd's:
    disorder,
    disintegration,
    destruction,
    decay,
    disease,
    death,
    doom,

then we have to ask the questions:

Is all same-sex desire and activity
necessarily doom-laden,
even if *some* may be?

Is not *some* heterosexual desire and activity
doom-laden,
though of course not *all* is sinful?

[contd. from previous page]

There are more questions:

1   Do we not too easily use the words
      'unnatural' and 'disgusting'
when what we really mean is
      'unfamiliar' and 'disturbing'?

It is easy to think of examples:

      a black face in nineteenth-century Cumbria,
      an exotic aroma from a restaurant,
      an extraordinary sexual technique
         which demands *very* supple limbs.

2   Is not the 'abnormal' best thought of as
      the statistically unusual or rare?

3   Do we not easily project on to others
      fears of chaos that are
         understandable,
         valid,
         but possibly unreasonable?

And does not increasing familiarity
with what previously has been unknown
      slowly calm us down,
      and even make us laugh?

[part of a sequence on pp 151-154]

4   Are we not *all* perplexed by the way
in which *all* human sexuality is disturbing?

We lose control:

    passion,
    orgasm,
    childbirth.

We make a mess:

    blood,
    semen.

We fear disease,

    so easily transmitted sexually.

We fear death,

    either from such disease,
    or in giving birth.

And we trust the tenderest parts of our anatomy
to another human being,

    sensitive to thrill and pleasure.
    porous to bacteria and viruses,
    vulnerable to damage.

Most of us learn to negotiate the rapids
    rather than refuse to get into a canoe.

And is there good reason to deny some of us
    a differently coloured canoe?

[part of a sequence on pp 151-154]

5   How do we understand the opposite of 'disorder',
           of the civil disorder of rioting,
           or of sexual variants of the same?
       What is it to be 'ordered'?

       Is it to have everything precisely
           'in order', 'in place'?
       Is it to be like an obsessively organized kitchen
           or filofax?

       Is it to follow exactly every detail of a recipe,
           and allow no place for flair?

       Is it to say that only our behaviour and customs
       are right and proper?

       Is it to have everything planned in advance,
           down to the last detail?

       (Is there somewhere lurking in the religious attic
           of our minds a notion of God like that?)

       We may feel that the only alternative is chaos.

       So, is there a 'universal grain' in the universe?

       And if so, how do we discern it?

                                    [part of a sequence on pp 151-154]

5   [continued]

Granted that 'blueprints' for motor cars
    and 'instructions' for their safe use are necessary,
does that describe every human enterprise?

(Even blue prints on paper are giving way to
    multi-coloured impressions on screens.)

Does everything have its 'pre-ordained' purpose,
'ordered' - both 'designed' and 'commanded' -
    by some celestial 'mastermind'?

(It would have to be 'master' wouldn't it?)

Is there but one 'fore-ordained' pattern
    that 'fits' everyone and everything,
    off the peg rather than made to measure?

Is 'order' a single static pattern
    or a variety of patterns
    seeking a moving harmonic relationship
    with one another?

Maybe a dynamic exchange
    between recognizable continuities
    and unpredictable risk
        is *inherent* in the 'nature' of things?

Do we not live in an open system
    rather than a closed one,
    open, that is, to
        change,
        growth,
        new patterns,
        new purposes?

[part of a sequence on pp 151-154]

If sex is 'naturally' about 'going forth and multiplying',
   it can of course seem 'unnatural' to be barren,
   to be infertile: it is not 'nature's' way.

In the past, to be barren was to be ashamed.
   If you were a woman, it was your fault.
   If you were a man and castrated,
     you were automatically without power or status
     in the matter of property, inheritance, and children.

Even today, for the fertile to choose to be childless
   is often felt to be selfish,
while to discover that you are infertile
   provokes pity rather than displeasure.

We may grant the *biological* precedence of reproduction
   (if cautious about too much 'multiplying'),
and its statistical 'normality',
but look for a precedence of value
   in two characteristics of sex-at-its-best:

intimacy	the desire to draw close to
	and be united with another;
creativity	the openness to change, to the future,
	to becoming more creative people
	because we are together
	than we were separately
	before we knew each other.

This is to be *pro-creative*, and includes
   the hospitality of a shared home;
   the pooling of talent in a business project;
   the encouragement of each other's singularity;
   the calling forth of self-giving love.

If not to be 'fertile', this is certainly to be 'fruitful'.

What do these phenomena have in common?
  Smallpox
  Earthquakes
  Sexual arousal
  Senility
Yes, they're all *natural*.

What do these phenomena have in common?
  Vaccines
  Bridges
  Viagra
  This book
Yes, they're all *unnatural*, or artificial.

So,
  there is no direct relationship
  between 'natural' and 'good'.

PS   This book may be bad,
         but that will be so
           if it is badly written,
           if the arguments are shoddy,
           if it encourages wrong-doing.
             (Some will think it does.)
         But it will not be bad
           simply because it is, as all books are,
           a human construct
           and not according to
           some supposed order of nature.

You cannot *prescribe* what another person
   should or must consider
'natural', genetically determined,
'normal', corresponding to social expectations.

You can apply such attributes as
   normal - abnormal,
   natural - unnatural,
   healthy - sick,
to yourself,

but you cannot *force your judgment*
   on those who describe themselves differently.

Such self-descriptions should be
   respected unconditionally,
while remaining open to being
   questioned courteously,
and being reminded that individuals
   are also members of social groupings
   with values that individuals are invited to
   adopt generously.

Conflicts should be resolved by
   negotiation through dialogue.

The musical note that is sounded by
  the spiritual,
  the creative,
  the sexual,
may be the same,
  though in different octaves.

Perhaps we treat as 'normal'
  only those chords we are used to,
  that sound harmonious to our ears,
each person in a relationship contributing a note
  that goes well with the other's.

If unusual chords are sounded,
  most people say Ouch:
  that is discordant
  (and therefore wrong?).

Do they try and forbid such music,
  denying it even the name of music?

But some people may be saying,
  I have been waiting all my life to hear this sound.
  I *recognize* it, deep within me, as mine.

The new resonance gives me *joy*.

What is a bodily organ *for*?

One purpose with a blueprint from long ago?
  (Mechanistic)

Many purposes, with an inbuilt
  (given, 'created' if you like)
  potential for that which is new,
  for that which has never happened before?
  (Holistic)

If the second,
  the whole is greater than the sum of the parts,
  and each whole is but part of a greater whole.

So, what are *mouths for*?
  Chewing?
  Spitting?
  Biting?
  Grunting?
  Speaking?
  Speaking Shakespeare?
  Kissing?

Historically,
  not all these functions were 'discovered' on day one.

And human inventiveness may not yet have dried up.

Do we not in *a variety of ways*
  already chew, spit, bite, etc.

Even the French may not have had the last word
  about kissing ...

'It's disgusting.'

This is the Yuk factor in discussion about sex,
  and very powerful it is.

Strong emotion makes rational discussion impossible,
  never more so than when matter is 'out of place',
  especially squishy matter,
  and linked without a second thought
  to dirt and the fear of disease and death.

'Dirty' money has to be 'laundered',
  not only dirty sheets
    (And how do they become dirty?)

So easy to have that 'gut' reaction
  that money and sex taint us.

After counting the coins from the charity envelopes -
  you don't know who's touched them -
  wash your hands.

After touching your genitals -
  even in the smallest room cleansed by toilet ducks -
  wash your hands.

What is your reaction
  (reaction, not considered response)
  to this question:
After sexual intercourse, do you feel
  that you have had a bath
  or that you need a bath?

Do you *value* faeces as compost?
  (Which, to come full circle, is to increase fertility.)

You can't be fertile - or fruitful - without muck.

The sense of what is clean and what is dirty
   varies from culture to culture.

(Each culture has its 'purity code',
   which may or may not have universal application,
   which may or may not be used to exclude people.)

To eat pig is by some regarded as unclean,
   and is therefore taboo.

Now I may be revolted (Yuk) by a film of a pig abattoir,
   but my disgust does not last long enough
   to make me give up eating bacon.

Eating bacon has never revolted me
   and has never made me ill.
On the contrary I have pleasurable memories,
   not least of cooking smells in the open air.

But I might be persuaded to give up eating bacon -
   because of the treatment of pigs;
   because of the ecological well-being of the planet;
   because the weather is hot and the fridge is broken;
   because it strains my digestive system.
These would be *reasons* -
   which is more than can be said for 'Yuk'.

By contrast,
   the very thought of oysters revolts me:
   this is because they make me ill.
Not even their supposed aphrodisiac properties
   can budge my stance on this issue.
But simply because that is my personal reaction,
   I try not to over-react
   and dismiss all oyster-eaters as immoral.

[part of a sequence, pp.161-164]

So, beware the connections,
   clean means good;
   dirty means bad.

Ask yourself how often you make that link
   when faced with
      unfamiliar smells,
      soggy litter,
      grubby clothes,
      unswept floors.
There may or may not be reason to fear disease.
   Think about it.

Recognize how every society has its rules about
   what is clean and what is dirty.
These rules create divisions and exclusions
   and always work against those on the margins.
The convictions run so deep and powerfully
   that those who are 'clean' and 'good'
   come to believe that certain kinds of behaviour
   simply do not exist among them.
And if, awful horror, an exception occurs,
   the offending person is separated
   from the rest of the community,
   either by incarceration and isolation
   or by exclusion and exile.

The powers that be in some African countries,
   not least in the churches,
   claim that same-sex behaviour does not occur there,
   that by definition it is a sign of western decadence ...

The story is told of a Jewish woman who told her parents
   that she was lesbian.
   'You can't be: you're Jewish.'
Scouring the family tree they found a remote Smith.
   'Ah, that's where it got in ...'

[part of a sequence, pp.161-164]

Clean and good, dirty and bad.
  Keep thinking about it.

The definitions are a habit,
  never mentioned,
  never questioned.

A habit as ingrained as 'dirt'
  embedded in the skin of fingers.

Think of the range of buckets, mops, and cloths
  of the average household of industrial England.

They are kept apart in places of their own.
They are kept apart from one another,
  if they have to clean away very dirty dirt.
Their purpose is skirted by euphemism.
Some are not even given house-room,
  but reside on hooks in out-houses.

Easy enough to transfer the emotion
  from mops to the mop-headed.
The mechanisms are in place
  for division, exclusion, separation, stigma.
She cannot be 'entertained' as 'one of us'.

[part of a sequence, pp.161-164]

All very comforting for those
  who have defined themselves as clean.
All very disturbing for the clean
  whose superficial belief
  may be in Jesus as a good teacher of morals.

Jesus crosses the boundaries of
  clean and dirty, pure and impure.
He touches the untouchables.
He *includes* them in a new community
  where the old rules are irrelevant to belonging.

You may be barren,
you may be dirty,
  but you belong,
  and you are not automatically in the wrong.

Jesus touched men with sores on their skin
  and women whose blood was flowing,
whose fluid matter was trespassing.

Jesus declared that all foods were clean,
  a stunning revolutionary statement and action
  that his followers found too shocking to absorb -
    at least at first.

(The stories tell of Peter needing a vision some years on,
  and hearing a command to kill and eat
  the comprehensive collection of animals
  let down in a sheet from heaven.)

Food was the issue that focused controversy
  in the first couple of generations after Jesus.
Christian Jews were in disagreement with other Jews,
  and were taken beyond the old confines:
Gentiles could become followers of Jesus
  without obeying the rules about food.

[part of a sequence, pp.161-164]

If food was a focus of controversy
   in the first generation,
same-sex relationships is a focus of controversy
   in the umpteenth generation.

Heterosexual Christians are in disagreement
   with homosexual Christians,
even denying that 'homosexual' and 'Christian'
   can be mentioned in the same breath.

Some of them are now being taken
   beyond the old confines of sex regulations
into accepting that homosexual people
   do not have to become
   (or pretend to become)
   heterosexual people
   before they can be accepted
   as members of the Christian community.

The old way - a couple of generations ago - was:

   Appearances are what count, dear boy.

They hadn't thought of the word 'spin' in the thirties,
   though the practice was current and dodgy,
     then as now.

Do your duty,
   get married,
   and keep to yourself whatever homosexual feelings
     you may have from time to time.

6
GOING WRONG

When is it wrong to have sex?

When it is an act of

violation,
  which is emotional and/or physical violence-abuse;

trespass,
  which is to intrude, invade,
  enter without invitation;

>   (Question: In our capitalist society,
>   is trespass against a person worse than
>   trespass against a person's property?)

or, as another way of putting it, an act of

power misused,
  which may be one or more of these kinds of power:

>   physical strength;
>   subtle manipulation;
>   sexual attractiveness;
>   money;
>   charisma;
>   public office,
>   e.g. police, clergy, teachers;

when by our actions we show that

we prefer simple solutions and actions
  and refuse to acknowledge
  the complexity of human beings;

we fall prey to lies and cruelty
  and refuse to acknowledge
  the need for truth and tenderness.

'I've got you where I want you.'

I dominate.
You submit.

This is usually visualized as a man raping a woman -

but it may also be a man raping a man

or indeed and alas, a child.

(Note: 'a man raping a man'
may be the only useful definition of 'sodomy'.)

This is male sexuality at its most disordered.
It combines
the thrill of mounting * sexual desire,
the excitement of humiliating
an enemy or subordinate,
the pleasure of inflicting pain.

(* Pun intended)

Such an atmosphere, if not the practice, is not unknown in
barracks at the initiation of recruits,
villages and towns as soldiers subdue them,
so-called fraternities at the admission of freshmen,

and any other environment that is
structured for
ruthlessness,
violence,
unbridled competition,
and controlled by
a strict hierarchy of command.

'You are merely an object for my own pleasurable use.'

A series of objects.
A sequence of anonymous encounters.
A box of paper tissues.

Each is disposed of without a moment's thought.

A sex life without
  continuity,
  connection,
  direction,

a refusal to allow sex its gift of enhancing the future:

  you are cut off from that possibility
  if you have already decided
  that you will never meet again.

There may be mutual consent,
  but human beings notoriously collude
    (I mis-typed that 'collide',
    but that too is true)
  in mutually destructive behaviour.

We tend to exploit and trivialize one another
  in ways that are
    subtle,
    hidden,
    habitual.
  and we soon forget that we are doing so.

This using of one another as objects
  may be the only useful definition of 'fornication'.

(PS A one-night stand may catch you out. See p. 183)

       10 June

'You are perfect and can meet my every need.'

This is the temporary marvel and eventual snare
  of romantic love.

To be 'in love' is to be
  ensnared,
  trapped,
  bewitched.
It is to wander around in a dream.

The other is an idol
  whose image fills every waking thought.
The mind's eye projects but one picture
  to fill the whole frame.

Too much is expected of the other,
  expectations that are impossible to fulfil.
Truth is betrayed.
Inloveness lies.
  It says 'I love you,'
  but it means, 'I lust after you,'
  or, 'I need your affection'.

Sooner or later lovers wake up to such truths.
  The illusion shatters.
  The spell is broken.
  The castle in the air crumbles.
Then it is usually separate paths
  with recrimination and bitterness at worst,
  with respect and affection at best.
(The truth-telling line is: 'I'm fond of you, but ...')
Or the two begin to learn how genuinely
  to love and be loved.

Sexual abuse by clergy was believed to be very rare.
  Perhaps it still is - at least in extreme forms.
  But we are not so sure.
Until recently bishops have colluded with the silence.
  They have placed individual careers
  and institutional reputation
  above truth and justice.
They have sided with the powerful
  and closed their ears to the cries of the oppressed.

If the atmosphere of an institution is such that it is
  embarrassing to talk about sex,
  unacceptable to admit to sexual feelings and arousal,
  against the rules to have sexual intercourse,
it is not altogether surprising that
  a potential for tenderness
  turns into an actuality of violence.

If all the passion is put into public performance
  and none into intimate relationships,
the public style detaches role from people,
  and the private reality detaches sex from meaning.
In both ways,
  power is separated from love.

NB
When the present Roman Catholic Archbishop of
  Liverpool was interviewed on his appointment,
he said that he had never had a conversation
  about contraception with a lay person.
Astounding until you remember that lay people
    either confess in the ritual of penitence
    or go their own way
knowing that they cannot have a conversation
  that is a genuine dialogue.
The silence of oppression once more descends.

There has been too much silence about sexual abuse,
  of children, of women, and even of men.
The innocent cannot believe that such things happen,
  apart, perhaps, from occasionally and sporadically.
(Actually, thousands of women were raped in Bosnia
  in the early nineties- and, as I write, Kosovo?)
The offenders keep quiet
  and try to get away with their crime.
The victims feel ashamed and powerless.
  They internalize the awfulness
  and come to believe themselves to be awful.
  And if you feel you are bad,
  you cannot show what the buried anger is like,
  either in words or with fists.

In war, soldiers are the guilty ones.
  They 'wipe out' people along with the villages.
  They conspire together to act and to keep silent.
'They said they would kill me if I didn't.'
  That was not a woman about to be raped,
  but a soldier about his peers.
Men have training and permission
  in using guns to kill when in a highly excited state.
Is it any wonder they use their other 'weapon'?

The circumstances of war give the opportunity
  for systematic and organized abuse.

Penetration separated from tenderness
  is experienced as lethal excitement.

'Words of the powerful in the land -
    haranguing, harassing, beating down,
    sly and clever, leaving the hearers dumb -
    words no longer heartfelt,
    their birth in the wordsmith's forge long forgotten,
    cruel now, and hard.
The poor, deprived of their language,
    rich oral language of their particular place,
    robbed of words that have meaning,
    stolen by peddlers of distortions and lies:
    the oppressed turn in on themselves and they howl -
    and the only way to relate is to hit.
A few, stung by the same hurting,
    search for words
    that can bring to birth
    fresh beauty, clarity, and truth.
They seek 'con-solation',
    that we may be 'warmed in the sun together',
    words alive and shimmering between us,
    sensuous words, full of passion,
    words charged with sexual power,
    enfleshed by throat and tongue and lips,
    engodded words creating and making love.'

Source: Jim Cotter, *Pleasure, Pain, and Passion*, Cairns Publications, 2nd edition, 1993, p. 85

May we repent,
  those who do these things
   and those who collude with them:

we kill animals for anything but food,
we relish the slaughter,
we exterminate whole species ...

we torture, sexually excited, in interrogation rooms,
we rape on city streets ...

we are men who force our pleasure
and leave women humiliated and exhausted,
  discarding them without a second thought ...

we peddle pornography
  that shows contempt and hatred,
  that hardens its practioners against intimacy,
  that exposes them to disease,
  that throws them out when their looks fade ...

we are religious fanatics
  who hate the flesh
  and seek to punish those different from ourselves ...

May the oppressed rise up with anger and compassion,
shaming those who do these things
  and those who collude with them,
offering to those whose hearts are changed
  the burning heat of forgiveness,
and together finding words
  for those who have had no voice of their own ...

May the oppressor and oppressed within each one of us
  begin by turning face to face ...

Source: Jim Cotter, *Pleasure, Pain, and Passion*, Cairns Publications, 2nd edition, 1993, pp. 85-6

'In repentance for thoughts, words, and deed:

hating the flesh
loathing the feminine
unleashing desire
withdrawing with hate
raping the earth
bruising a lover
roaming restlessly
wasting time
living a lie
hiding behind words
burning with zeal
ignoring the other
dominating the other
possessing the other
humiliating the other
discarding the other
scything whole peoples
scapegoating the powerless
refusing to play
glowing with self-righteousness ...'

Source: Jim Cotter, *Pleasure, Pain, and Passion*, Cairns Publications, 2nd edition, 1993, p. 86

Addiction to self-destructive forms of behaviour
   can be powerful and become all-pervasive.
It is a kind of death-wish.
For some people who grew up
   realizing with discomfort and even horror
   that they were physically and emotionally attracted
   to others of their own sex,
   and knowing that to admit it
   would result in being shamed,
a script was etched deep into their very being:
   you are not of worth,
   you do not deserve being treated with dignity,
   it would be better if you hadn't been born.
So, and especially with sexually transmitted diseases,
   you absorb the message of hatred
   and internalize it:
   you come to believe that you deserve
   what is coming to you.
Now, if we all received our deserts,
   human life would no longer exist at all.
And if we received what is due to us,
   those who are greedy and malicious and violent
   would suffer more than anybody else.
(How easy it is to forget -
   and that is because we haven't got beyond the theory -
   that sexual wrong has never been high on the list
   of Christian wrongdoing.)

Desperate for tenderness,
   you look for it *everywhere*,
   and you look for it from *anybody*.

You are, without realizing it,
   'beside' yourself
   (probably with rage
   at being cheated of your birthright),
   not at all 'centred',
   not at all 'grounded'.
A feather could knock you over.

It is precisely at such moments
   that the con-artist lurks
   who is well versed in recognizing
   the look in your eyes
   and the posture of your body.

Desperate need is blind,
   is not streetwise enough
   to steer clear of the predator
   out for cash - or revenge.
Desperate need cannot distinguish
   between spring water and salt water.
The thirst is overwhelming.

Lemming like you trot into the lair.
Your life is literally in another's hands.
Before you know it,
   you have been relieved of your wallet.
Before you feel it,
   you have been wounded by knife point.

You have no power of yourself to help yourself.
'Angels and ministers of grace defend us.'

Source: *Hamlet* I. iv. 20

7
COMING RIGHT

Ah, those regrets,
   the might have beens.

You can pinpoint the place
   and clearly remember the other person.

Taunton ... Auckland ... Chamonix ...

Somehow the opportunity was missed
   for shared delight and pleasure
   in the great variety of creation.
Energy was moving, one towards the other,
   but tentatively, uncertainly,
   body language confused.
But contact was not made -
   through fear perhaps,
   through lack of confidence in the truth of touch,
   through the inner voice of disapproval.

And it needn't have been about sex.

It might have been
   conversation,
   laughter,
   embrace,

a contribution of happiness
   to the world's well-being.

(And we wouldn't have regrets
   unless we also remembered the good times ...)

Sex as survival strategy:
Scattered sex as a gut reaction
   to the traps of a hostile society,
   rather than a considered response.
If you breathe an atmosphere of
   rejection, violence, and alienation,
you imbibe those very attitudes -
   which in your best moments you wish to counter.
You 'take up' with people
   and 'drop' them
   when you become close enough to begin to be vulnerable,
   and for others around you to notice.
You do violence to your own needs for
   trust, intimacy, leisure, play -
   all of which take time and need safety.
But where is continuity possible
   if you are young and still live at home,
   or you are a student in a far from soundproof bedsit,
   or the only public spaces for meeting others
     reek of sexual competition?
So it is difficult for sexual activity as such
   to find its own level in a relationship,
outer and inner forces combining
   to make it more likely than not
   that your sexual life will be a series of
   relatively anonymous and sporadic encounters.
Social pressures split people into fragments,
   or at least into tight and sealed compartments,
and even when a minority forms a pressure group,
   it does not have a common history to hold it together,
   and its own identity is not yet secure enough
     to keep it together when tensions inevitably arise.
Sex in this context is not only a strategy for survival
   but a celebration of resistance to cultural norms.
In both personal and social spheres this is changing,
   as both couples and groups do stay together.
But much of the territory is still unmapped.

Meet the cruisers in the open democracy
    of park and woodland:

where the young score frequently
    and the old are ignored;
where the streetwise keep their wits about them
    as night falls;
where there is the excitement of the hunt,
    the glint in the eye of the 'stalker'
    and the knowing smile on the face of the 'prey';
where the lost souls wander, empty-eyed;
where anonymity prevents the openness
    that would be too hard to bear;
where students seek to supplement their income
    now that grants are no longer enough;
where members of the tribe gossip, recommend, and warn;
where professional people search furtively,
    their public roles forcing discretion
    as the necessary part of valour;
where married men can spend a few minutes
    on the way home without raising suspicion;
where the young with no place of their own
    look for someone with safe space to share;
where fleeting affirmation is better than nothing at all,
    but all too often fades to the grey of dust and ashes;
where there are many 'tourists',
    who gaze with glazed eyes,
but few 'pilgrims',
    who connect and communicate with what they see.

NB
If sex has meaning only in context,
    it does not follow that
    all sporadic sex is without context,
    nor that that context is inevitably negative.

'One night stands':
  it is a phrase from the world of entertainment
  transferred to the world of sex.
Think of the former
  and ask how it might apply to the latter.

NB Note the difference between an *analogy* and an *allegory*.
      The intention of an analogy is
        to show how some points of comparison fit.
      The intention of an allegory is
        to make *every* point of comparison fit.
We are dealing here with an analogy:
  analogies make you think;
  allegories confirm you in what you already think.

1   You have to draw close to strangers quickly.
       You may have devised certain protective techniques
        but the armour-plated cannot communicate.
       To communicate you have to risk being vulnerable.
2   You have to woo your audience.
       A warm-up may be similar to fore-play.
3   You may fail to make a connection,
       the jokes may fall flat,
       you may not rise to the occasion.
       The evening will be unmemorable,
        turning to dust and ashes,
        leaving a sour taste in the mouth.
4   You may turn 'play' into a power 'game'.
       You may mesmerize an audience.
       You may bewitch with the magic of wordcraft.
       You may use the techniques of the campaign trail
        of politician or evangelist.
       Of course your audience,
        enjoying being dependent,
        giving up responsibility,
        even being abused,
          may love to 'have it' so.

If there are no continuities,
  how do you avoid disintegration?
  how can you be fully alive and present
    for the new audience in the next city?

Yet there *are* sexual relationships occupying a territory
  between abuse or ashes at one end
  and monogamy or celibacy at the other.

What name do we give them?
  Serial monogamy?
  A bisexual person's relationships with one other
    of each gender?
  One-night stands which take off?

Are there circumstances in which 'sex only once'
  is not diabolic but symbolic?
  where repetition would betray
    that which the sex is symbolic of:
  the 'something more' that is primary
    and much more significant
    because deeper and long-lasting?
  where the Yes of sex affirms rather than denies
    a more profound Yes?

A seal on a friendship?
An affirmation of the other's value and worth
  as an embodied being?
An initiation for one whose virginity
  has been prolonged through fear and guilt?
A paradoxical affirmation
  of a primary vocation to solitude?

Think about it.

The question is answered No
   if the motive is a desperate and despairing need
     for a sense of identity,
   where a sexual response
     would be a cruel raising of hopes
     only to dash them.

However much the entertainer relishes applause,
   unless he or she has a clear sense of identity,
     of a place within self and society,
   one-night stands carry a high risk of disintegration,
     a constant succession adding to the peril.

There is another danger
   if there is no continuity and no relationship.

Sexual desire is powerful, exciting, pleasurable.
   If your first experiences of sexual contact
     are anonymous and furtive,
     with no possibility of love,
     and no social context in which love can grow,
   then guilt, fear, and shame
     rapidly become associated with sex,
       (a link made more solid
       by lack of sane and sensible sex education),
     along with the excitement and pleasure.

With repetition, a pattern is formed,
   pattern becomes habit,
   becomes fixation, addiction, compulsion.

Addiction rules where power is not contained by love.

And only love can break the cycle.

Where a sexual act occurs between two people
  with consent and with no obvious harm,
the law has no place,
  but discernment may be needed
  in terms of what is good, better, and best.
The good may be minimal.
But it is important to recognize that there is indeed good
  in the most unlikely circumstances.
There is pleasure and affirmation
  even in places of seemingly worthless waste.
There is at least the seed of goodness.
And that is there because the flesh is good,
  that bodies are good for us.
You may not see the seed because it is too small.
You may without realizing it be trampling on the seed.
  But you cannot destroy it.
There may be much more to be said,
  much more to be experienced of the goodness,
  much, much more that is better and best.
But we grow from recognizing the good,
  not from hating ourselves
  because we have not achieved the best.
The best -
  all that talk about ideals -
  can in practice be the enemy of the good.

That which is visually attractive
   and immediately available
   deceives in offering more than it can give.
It is the chief characteristic of golden calves -
   four legs or two –
   and other idols.

To experience too much or too many
   is to dissipate energy
   and to live on the surface:
its danger is to become
   dis-connected
   (because the lines of connection are weak and thin)
   dis-located
   (because you are never in one place long enough
     really to belong).

To seize for yourself,
   seeing whatever or whoever only in your own light,
   is to refuse to live with the unknown.

To take in too much without digestion
   is to risk mental and physical confusion and dis-ease.

To accumulate thoughts, possessions, people,
   is to be trapped by them,
   enclosed by them,
   weighed down by them.

The opposite is to be sprung from the trap
   (which is one of the root derivations of 'salvation').

Therefore
   prune, slim, deepen;
   become focused and centred;
   be connected and at home;
   live with uncontrollable mystery of the other.

Is it true that, for some,
    their sexuality is so bound up with their creativity
    that there is no sexual energy left over
    for the all-consuming passion of romance
    or for the all-consuming chores of domesticity?
There may be room for
    the unexpected gift of sexual embrace
    and for the steadiness of deep companionship,
and it may be for a sexual relationship
    in which the one who sacrifices most
    is the one who gives energy through sexual encounter
    that feeds the other's artistic creativity.

We have clear rules when we play games.
There may be an unwritten contract,
    even a referee.

Ask of intimate games,
    What are the rules?
    Will this game be a game
    of acting out or of feeling through?
    Will it be a game of fantasy or will it tell the truth?
    Does it allow for creative imagination?
    Does one of us have to lose,
    or is mutual enjoyment the prize?

Within the high boundaries of clear rules we can
    relax,
    trust,
    play,
    laugh.
As we approach the encounter,
    tenderness and shyness will dissolve the barriers.

Then the release of our power
    is for our passion and engagement,
    not for our force and violation.
We may be on the boundaries of pain and pleasure,
    we may be wild and uninhibited,
    love may bite (love-bites),
but we will not harm.

When is it right to have sex?

When sexual intercourse
  is 'sym-bolic',
    a 'joining together',
  not 'dia-bolic',
    a 'splitting apart'.

When there is a 'coursing' of energy 'between' two people,
  an 'inter-coursing'.

    (Notice the emphasis there:
    not on the act itself, of intercourse,
    but on the dynamic of the action, the inter-coursing.)

When two people
  draw close through *mutual* attraction,
    connect,
    become intimate,
    already feel as one,

  sexual union is then a matter of
    making love,
    deepening intimacy,
    healing wounds,
    strengthening bonds,
    creating that which is new,

  thus convincing them
    that only by staying together
    will a new future be nourished into being,
    and protected into growing.

Thus 'having sex' changes into 'making love',
   through both stillness and wildness,
   through both contemplation and action:

the *quieter* mode of
   being attentive to the other,
   indeed 'paying' attention,
   respecting the 'singular-ity' of the other,
   contemplating the other
   who will always be other,
   always 'distinctive',
   potentially 'distinguished',
   having the courage to draw close,
   and to stay close,
   to become intimate.

the *noisier* mode of
   passionate engagement,
   the 'passion' of sexual energy
   and the willingness to bear love's hurts,
   the 'engagement' of involvement and commitment,
   the desire for the unknown future
   that is being created.

If our sexual energies are to be directed towards
   intimacy and creativity,

we need

  time
    for mutual trust to grow;

  commitment
    into which we can relax;

  high boundaries,
    to protect the tender and vulnerable,
    which is our skin, our flesh, our love;

  shielding from the public eye -
    the privacy which is not necessarily secrecy;

  the play and laughter
    that comes from feeling safe about tomorrow;

  private (and secret) names
    that strengthen an intimate bond;

  leisure
    in which old wounds can be opened to a healing touch.

So we move towards valuing
  repeated acts of love-making,
  within a committed and faithful relationship
  which matures over time.

Sexual intercourse,
  in the broadest sense,
  comes into 'play'
  whenever we 'touch matter with love'.

The matter involved may be

  the body of another in human love-making;

  the soil of the earth in the hands of a gardener;

  the ingredients of a recipe for a cook;

  clay in the shaping fingers of a potter;

  words enfleshed by rhythm and resonance
    at the tip of a poet's pen.

It could be said that

  when intimacy and creativity

    are joined with matter,

      Holy Spirit is at work.

Officially the Roman Catholic Church now recognizes
   that our sexuality
     is an integral part of our humanity;
   that sexual intercourse
     has a positive value in uniting
     and bonding two people.
I think I am right in saying
   that it is only since 1950
   that official documents about marriage
   have mentioned the uniting power of sex.
But in Roman Catholic teaching
   this unitive meaning of sex
   is not to be separated from its procreative meaning.
Therefore any sexual act
   not open to the transmission of human life
   is thought to limit the total self-giving
     of one person to the other
   that is implicit in the unitive aspect
     of the marriage relationship.
Therefore contraception,
   and, even more, homosexual acts,
   cannot be approved in any circumstances.
Might it be possible to broaden out understanding
     of what it means to be *creative*,
   and recognize that it might mean more
     than simply to be *procreative*?
Perhaps *pro-creative*?

To be *pro-creative*
  is to approve of
  and to engage in
    acts which issue in the greater well-being
    of self, the other, and others (society as a whole).

Sexual desire can be open
  to such consequences as these:

1   Not only the binding together of two people,
        but the affirmation of the other's bodily being,
        the healing of the other's emotional wounds,
        the growth of the other towards maturity.

2   The releasing of creative energy
        to contribute to the greater good of the society
        of which both are part.

For most people,
  the primary and most committing creativity
  is indeed to be procreative,
  in the conceiving, birth, and nurture of children.

For some people the primary
  and for most people the secondary
  mode of creativity
  is in some form of art
    which may or may not be a solitary activity,
  and in some form of service,
    from the hospitality of a shared home
    to the enterprise of a shared endeavour.

Note that this approach says more than,
  Do what you want to do
  provided no one is harmed
  and no burden is placed on the community.
It points to acts that positively benefit the community.

Desires,
   whether for sex, power, wealth, possessions,
   are very powerful
and can be
   inordinate,
   excessive,
   disordered,
   enslaving.

Desires
   have their proper place,
   their right place,
     in the context of,
     held by,
     shaped by,
     directed by,
   the kind of loving goodwill
     that is intimacy
       in the private sphere
     and justice
       in the public sphere.

Thus power is contained
and desire itself transformed.

So it may be that human desires
   through prayer and struggle
   become aligned to the divine desire
   to be incarnated in us.
That it involves prayer
   acknowledges that this alignment is impossible
   without grace from beyond our ego selves,
   welling up from the depth of our true selves.
That it involves struggle
   acknowledges that we need
   the wisdom, guidance, and support
   of friends, family, and wider community.

In Christian thought and imagination
  sex and sin have been consistent bedfellows
  (as it were).
Indeed the two words have often seemed interchangeable.
We have reacted against that identification,
  but sometimes we have claimed that
  sex and sin have nothing to do with each other
  rather than *everything* to do with each other.
Now it is relatively easy to identify certain sexual acts
  and call them sinful -
  rape is the obvious example.
But there may also be a sense in which
  we can never escape sin for long.
And by sin I mean a pervasive atmosphere
  and a dense interconnected structure of activity
  which we breathe
  and in which we are all caught up.
Even the most wonderful moments of union
  are only that - moments.
They may be a foretaste of heaven,
  but they are only that - a foretaste.
There is nearly always what the French call 'tristesse',
  a post-coital sadness that the bliss is already fading,
  an inevitable wistfulness.
And that is sex at its best.
We have only to go on to remember
  that we are not yet wholly purged
  of self-centredness,
  of restlessness,
  of dissatisfaction.
Nevertheless,
  simply because some things that happen are not perfect
  does not mean that they are completely wrong ...

The journey towards sexual maturity
   is from 'need love' to 'gift love'.

As infants and children,
   we need to have our identity, worth, and security
     sufficiently affirmed.
At best such affirmation is partial,
   but if it is not *enough*,
     especially if it is seriously *deficient*,
we shall seek in our adult life
   some measure of what we lacked.
We shall look for more of 'the same'.

A man may, as they say, marry a woman like his mother
   (and not for his stomach's needs alone).
A man may seek identity from the 'father' in another man.
The relationship may be sexual at one level,
   therapeutic at another.
The wasteland may or may not be re-covered,
   the wounds of the past may or may not be healed.
The best chance occurs when both parties know
   that this healing process
     is a necessary part of their relationship,
   so that they are alert to mutual kindness.

What is being sought is
   more of *the same*,
     minimal in the past,
     being made up in the present.

Perhaps this is the 'homo' element
   in most intimate adult relationships,
whether with someone of the same sex or of the opposite sex.

It does not make the relationship immature,
   but it does describe an essential element in it.

Contrast the previous page with another reality,
sometimes in small measure at first,
becoming more characteristic in time.

This is the 'hetero' element in intimate adult relationships,
again, whether with the opposite or with the same sex.

This is the change, not complete, but recognizable,
from 'need love' to 'gift love'.
Each offers the other gifts from his or her *difference*.

A *measure* of intimacy -
which is not to decry it
or diminish its significance -
may be achieved through sameness.
Creativity needs the spark of *difference*.

And such 'difference',
such 'hetero-ness',
can be more characteristic of
many 'homosexual' relationships
than of
some 'heterosexual' relationships
that never move on
from their initial 'homo-ness'.

The language of that last sentence is hardly felicitous.
But I write these last two pages
to jolt our usual assumptions
and to make us *think*.

Source: A suggestion of Beau Stevenson in a discussion near Oxford in the
early nineties

So we may come to a deeper understanding
  of the virtue of 'chastity'.

It is not to be defined negatively as 'no sex'.

Rather is it a loving that has been
  pruned,
  refined,
  purified,
that has become
  accurate,
  truthful,
  non-possessive.

Need has been transfigured into gift.

It is characterized by an ability
  to give the other space
    even when feeling needy,
  to draw close to the other
    even when feeling afraid -

and, lest we pretend we can be
  totally giving *all* the time,
  an ability to receive the same courtesies in return.

NB

If we are invited to love others,
  what are the others invited to do?

(I think that is roughly something
  that W. H. Auden pondered.)

Some definitions of *chastity*;

> Emotional honesty.

> Non-possessive loving.

> Relationships pruned of self-centred-ness.

And here is one from the centre
   of the Roman Catholic Church ...

(Hold your breath
   and suspend prejudice
   that no good thing can come out of - er -
   was it Nazareth?
   is it Rome?)

'That spiritual energy
   capable of defending love
   from the perils of selfishness
   and aggression.'

Source: The Pontifical Council for the Family, quoted in 'The Truth and Meaning of Sexuality', *Catholic International*, vol. 7, nos. 4-5, April-May 1996, p. 202, with acknowledgement.

Part of the mystery of human sexuality
  is that it never yields all that it promises
  of union and creativity.
We are too muddled and mischievous,
  self-centred and seduced by lies,
  fragile and broken,
for our loving to be clear and truthful and whole.
We yearn for what is incomplete to be completed.
It is and always will be a fact of life.
The point is whether we complain or not.
Can we let the longing settle in the heart of us,
  maybe as a secret wound, however open?
Oases of milk and honey will have to be sufficient.
A sexual relationship may well give us
  more than we ever dreamed was possible,
but there may also be a strange and perplexing gift
  in the secret mystery of
  solitude, barrenness, emptiness,
  of the desert rather than of the oasis.
There is something waiting to be given
  in the midst of the hollow empty place.
As womb, it is a place which from time to time is filled,
  though not for every woman and not for always.
As emptiness, it is a place every human being comes to,
  and is challenged to respond to the ache of it.
Is it the place where, more than anywhere else,
  the divine love is encountered
  in quiet intimacy
  and surge of creative energy?
Such a gift cannot be demanded as of right,
  cannot be controlled,
  can only be prepared and waited for.
Those among God's spies who are artists and poets,
  scientists and inventors, godfriends, monks, and nuns
  perhaps know something of this truth.

It is a daring and awesome moment
  when one human being says to another,
    I promise to love you for the rest of my life,
  for each to say to the other,
    You are more important to me
    than anyone else in the world.

But first unpack the process that leads up to
  and beyond that moment.

There are three promises,
  each of them subtly but profoundly different.

Here is the first.

This is the promise that means,

  At this moment, here and now,
  I love you more than anyone else in the world,
    and I promise to work at
    deepening and expanding my love.
  But we are not yet ready
    to share a home,
   (and, some will want to add),
    to care for children.
  We are still learning how to love,
    learning what it is,
      not simply to know about each other,
    but much more what it is
      to *know* each other,
        embracingly,
        penetratingly.

[part of a sequence, pp. 203-207]

Here is the second promise.

I can now say to you more profoundly than before,
    after this time of knowing and loving,
    of learning and growing together,
    that I love you more than anyone else in the world.
I promise to share my worldly goods with you.
I promise to care for such children
    as may be entrusted to us.
I want to go on loving you and being loved by you
    so that it is only death that will ever separate us.

Here is the third promise.

Now that the children have grown up and left home,
    my renewed promise embraces a different courage.
I love you more than anyone else in the world,
    you have become to me as a soul-mate,
    so deep has our friendship become,
but my love for you now supports you
    in your own singular creative task.
I promise to give you sufficient room to breathe,
    to guard your deepest being.
I will begin to focus on the 'not yet'
    that will carry each of us beyond death.
I promise you the kind of love
    that is of two solitudes
    who border, touch, and greet each other.

NB

Those last two lines come from R. M. Rilke's letters
    to a young poet

[part of a sequence, pp. 203-207]

A few supplementary points:

1   Those three modes of promise
        may be made by the same two people
        as their love grows,

    the first characteristic of, say, age 16-28 -
        'knowing',

    the second characteristic of, say, age 28-49/56 -
        'nesting',

    the third characteristic of, say, age 49/56 onwards
        'not yet'.

    (The 'n' sounds are merely an aid to memory.)

    Or the promises may be made
        to two or three different people
        for the different stages of adult life.

[part of a sequence, pp. 203-207]

2   Promises are never easy to keep,
        and with the best of intentions,
        two people may find themselves
        saying to each other,

We have exhausted the meaning of our love.

Or,

We have caused each other pain,
    and we have not been able to dig deep enough
    to discover fresh resources of love
    that could contain and heal the hurt.

The agony is when the meaning and supply of love
    has run dry for one person,
  but still flows in the other.

[part of a sequence, pp. 203-207]

3   In these descriptions of love fulfilled,
          the balance is shifting within each stage,
          and from each stage to the next,

     from 'need' to 'gift';

     from 'dependency' and/or 'independence'
          to 'inter-dependence;

     from 'homo' to 'hetero'
          (in the sense defined on pp. 198-199)

     But there are no differences that matter
          ethically or spiritually
     between opposite-sex relationships
          and same-sex relationships.

[part of a sequence, pp. 203-207]

Some indicators of increasing commitment
  between two people:

    joint mortgage or rental agreement;
    joint bank account;
    drawing up of wills in each other's favour.

To establish each of those
  we usually need the oversight and assistance
  of those expert and publicly accountable
  in the worlds of law and finance.

Documents signed and witnessed
  place the relationship in the public domain
  and begin to signify to the partners
  and to those who know them
  that this relationship is uniquely special.

Such contracts, conforming to the law of the land,
  indicate to families, neighbours, friends, associates,
  that this relationship is primary and central
  to the lives of each partner.

Its inner shape may best be characterized by
  the mutuality of friendship,
but it has gone beyond the privacies and informality
  of friendship.
For many this is the moment of commitment
  to a partnership for life.

A public ceremony of covenant and blessing
  may mark the moment,
witnessed by those who are close to the partners
  and by those who represent the wider community,
and whose own relationship to them changes for ever,
  as it does after any rite of passage.

8
MAKING CHOICES

We invent categories to protect ourselves
    from insecurity and change.
But such classfications are always approximate
    and provisional at best.
We forget the variety of life,
    and that greater variety is a good thing.
Few people are 100% heterosexual,
    few are 100% homosexual.
We respond sexually (broad bodily sense)
    to many different men and women.
We respond sexually (narrower genital sense)
    to far fewer.

But in all our connections, all our relationships,
    we have to negotiate boundaries and activities
    with responsibility and care.
There are indeed rules,
    but guidelines in the form of challenging questions
    are more helpful than 'dead' lines of prohibitions.
Some of the latter may be necessary for extreme cases,
    but not necessarily including
'No sex anywhere but in heterosexual monogamous
    marriage,'
    or
'No same-sex activity anywhere at all.'

Rather, for example,
    'What kind of touch will increase love between us
        and not decrease it elsewhere?'
    'How, given the limitations of both of us,
        can we be vulnerable to each other without harm?'

Why do we think that rape is wrong?
    Do we judge it so
    because it causes immense harm
    or because God has revealed it to us as wrong in itself?
Well,
    revelation is not irrational:
    it commends itself to us
    only if we can discern a good reason.
'Because I say so'
    is the temporary refuge of the weary parent.
And much depends upon our notion of God,
    as arbitrary and despotic power,
    or as the power that continually works
    to bring order out of chaos,
    to create and not to destroy.
So we discern the rightness or wrongness of an action
    by asking where revelation and reason join.
The process looks at the circumstances of the action,
    the motives of those involved,
    and not least the consequences.
This often involves us in hard choices,
    challenging us to decide which of two wrongs
    will lead to the worse consequences,
    or which of two rights will lead to the greater good.
We may decide that some acts are always wrong
    and blameworthy
and others are always wrong
    but not always the most blameworthy choice.
We may decide that certain actions are always right
    and praiseworthy,
and others are always right
    but not always the most praiseworthy choice.

A traditionalist approaching sexual ethics:
'I agree there should be no discrimination
  on the grounds of sexual orientation alone.
But, biologically, male and female are polar opposites,
  and this implies marriage and nowhere else
  as the place for sexual intercourse.'
This claim is usually backed by an appeal
  to the order of creation given by God,
  and summed up in Genesis 1.27-28.

Thus marriage. With celibacy its status varies.
For Roman Catholic and Orthodox Churches,
  it is clearly the norm for the unmarried,
  and therefore for all homosexual people.
For Protestant Churches,
  singleness is a state which is pre-marriage,
  and so is assumed to be one of sexual abstinence,
  and as marriage is the only acceptable structure
    for sexual intercourse,
  in practice these churches take the same view
    of homosexual acts as do the others.
Some would add that the institution of marriage
  is called into question, even degraded,
  by same-sex partnerships,
  whether quietly tolerated or openly accepted.
Thus the blessing of such partnerships is prohibited.
However, if a homosexually-orientated person
  is persuaded to contract a heterosexual marriage
  (to be 'cured', to have children,
  to become socially and ecclesiastically acceptable),
is not such a person likely to distort self
  and to harm the partner to such a marriage?
And why in any case is a stable, faithful, lasting same-sex
  partnership thought to denigrate marriage?
Is the real reason a suspicion of pleasure
  and a prejudice that such a relationship
  is bound to be selfish?

If your church wished formally to adopt
  a liturgy for the blessing of a same-sex partnership,
would you
  welcome it and vote for it?
  be uneasy and abstain?
  vote against, denounce all such relationships,
  and seek to expel lesbian and gay people
    from your church?
  vote against, and if the vote went the other way,
    leave, and join another church?
    seek to take others with you?
    seek to set up a church claiming to be the true one?
Churches have often made the distinction between
  matters on which it is legitimate
    to hold varying opinions,
    e.g. dress, use of money, declarations of war,
  and matters of fundamental significance,
    where boundaries are fixed and clear.
So it is continually likely
  over matters of belief and behaviour
  that this question will arise:
Do certain opinions and practices
  put the unity of this church at risk?
The question above is one of these.

If you are very clear about your beliefs,
  The Truth, capital 'T', mattering above all,
  you will tend to put clear water
  between yourself and those whom you oppose.
If you are very clear that living with disagreement
  is both possible and very important,
  you will tend to point out that struggles
    muddy the waters for a while,
  but that we grow when we search together,
  alert for fresh insights,
  aware that as we take the time to do this,
  some will continue to suffer from discrimination.

Think a little more about this distinction between
   fundamental criteria that apply in all contexts
   and are of lasting importance,
   and moral advice specific to particular contexts.
Those contexts include
   the people concerned,
   each with his or her singularity,
   and the local cultures, structures, and traditions,
   political, social, and religious.
Each of these contexts has the right to be respected,
   but none of them can be transferred entire
   to other contexts.
An inevitable problem arises when
   previously closed moral environments
   are influenced by different environments.
This is the situation we find ourselves in
   because of frequent travel and instant contact.
We have to work much harder than we did before
   at criteria which are indispensable, comprehensive,
   and, if possible, universal.
We can see the process at work in declarations
   of human rights, human responsibilities,
     and spiritual values.
It seems there is no alternative to this task,
   requiring patience, respect, and thoughtfulness.
We are looking for ways in which
   ethical discernment, advice, and axioms
   can take seriously
     new factual knowledge,
     biblical and other religious traditions,
     contemporary values and norms
     notions of individual and common good,
     estimates of consequences,
   and refuses to take seriously only one of these,
     e.g. 'proof' texts, immemorial custom,
     'common sense', empirical observation.

If love comes first, not rules,
      our questions are these:

1	Not	What does the law permit?
	But	What does it mean here and now
		to love this person?
		What does love require?
		What kind of touch will enhance love?

2	Not	What breaks God's laws sexually?
	But	What behaviour violates our integrity
		in the presence of a God of love?

3	Not	What does this verse of Scripture say?
	But	What is the Spirit of God saying to us now
		in the light of the whole Bible,
		more particularly in the light of the Bible
		at its best,
		and in the light of
		the experience of our ancestors,
		recent new knowledge,
		contemporary discernment?

After all, Luke (12.57) reports Jesus as asking,
  Why do you not judge for yourselves
    what is right?

And we may not quite understand what Paul meant
  when he said that we are to judge angels,
but if so, as he continued,
  we are all the more to judge matters
    concerning this life.
(1 Corinthians 6.3)

And *that* is to bring in the witness of the Bible at its best
  against the Bible at its worst.

.

9
EXERCISING AUTHORITY

Domination Hierarchy
   define and exclude,
   practise distance and separation,
   stand above others,
   exercise power over others,
   inhabit intimidating and costly
      clothes and houses.

Servant 'hierarchies'
   accept and include,
   practise association and connection,
   stand alongside others,
   empower others,
   inhabit welcoming and ordinary
      clothes and houses.

Power over others is used reluctantly,
   protecting the boundaries within which
      mutuality can flourish,
   framing and keeping laws that give
      justice and intimacy a chance.

The movement and intention is always
   away from power over
   towards power shared
   and in the end to power given away,
from overpowering
   to empowering
   to vulnerability.

We need to be honest when we approach
  any source, any beginning, any foundation
    that carries weight,
    which bears *authority* for us.
We have to ask what in truth is from
  the source, the *author*.
We have to remember that what is given to us as from
  divine authority, the ultimate source,
is mediated
  through people and language,
  through custom and culture.

So rules are the contemporary customs
  practised by a given community,
  based on authority,
  backed by sanctions,
    both formal laws
    and informal opinion.
Such customs are usually taken for granted:
  rarely are assumptions questioned.

When nearly everybody accepts them,
  when external authority has been internalized,
  the occasional person who acts against them
    is either shunned by the neighbourhood
    or punished for disobeying the law,
    or both.

When a substantially increasing minority acts against them
  their assumed universality is challenged,
  formerly accepted laws fall into disrepute,
  we delve again into our sources,
  we ask questions arising from new knowledge,
  we argue and debate,
  and eventually we change the rule book.

We have a choice.

Do you believe in a judgmental condemning God
(not, note, a wise God exercising discerning judgment),
who consigns to everlasting punishment and pain
    the vast majority of the human race,
preserving only those few who think that God
    has chosen them for special favour?
You have to recognize that there is plenty in the Bible
    that supports that point of view,
    even in the Gospels.

Or do you hold a radically different point of view,
    one that is in conflict with the first
    within the very pages of the Bible itself?
God *specially* favours those
    who are put down by the ones
    who think only they themselves are special.
God identifies with those
    who the superior classify as 'sinners'
    who are pushed to and over the edge
        by the religious and political élites of the day,
    who dominate the vast majority, the stigmatized,
        the poor, maimed, diseased;
        the prostitutes, tax collectors, slaves, women;
        the differently coloured, the sexually different.
God is a com-passionate God,
    a suffering-with-us God,
    a long-suffering God,
    a God of *unlimited* forgiveness
    a pain-bearing God,
who keeps on loving until
    even the wealthy and powerful are shamed
    into accepting the embrace of those
    they have treated as outcasts.
God is like the Jesus who embodied such love,
    and in God there is nothing that is unlike Jesus.

Power is exercise by those
   who uphold the letter of the current law,
   who have access to funds from the wealthy
      (who always have a vested interest in the status quo)
      and from the majority
      (who always fear change),
   and who therefore use subtle - and not so subtle -
      techniques of financial blackmail.

Authority is exercised by those

who by their office have power to say No to bullies;

who use that power only as a last resort;

who include those affected by a possible No
   in the discussions that lead up to decisions;

who seek a greater Yes beyond the necessary No;

who are aware of how easy it is to misuse power;

who are themselves willing to be identified
   with those who have least power in any conflict;

who create hospitable places
   where conflicts can be contained,
   where dialogue can be encouraged,
   where people feel safe enough to express their feelings
      and tell their stories,
      and relaxed enough to listen to others,
   where each respects the convictions of others,
   where those of different positions are all open to change,
   where humour is never far away;

who bear the cost of self-giving love
   and self-authenticating truth.

All churches have some appeal to authority
  that is not independent of the Scriptures,
    but is not in practice Scripture alone:
      there is always someone to interpret where authority is
      accepted, even if simply that of the individual reader.
For Roman Catholics,
  there is the Magisterium, centred on the Pope.
For the Orthodox,
  there are the church fathers of the first centuries.
For Protestants,
  there are varied appeals to synods, bishops,
  professors, pastors, and congregations.
What is relatively new is that
  statements from 'authority' may be 'official'
  but they can no longer be enforced.
The 'consensus of the faithful' cannot be achieved
  simply by prescription and exhortation.
Some leave the churches
  (no longer afraid of hell-fire).
Some silently disobey
  and remain members for other reasons.
This is not unity and risks diversity run riot into chaos.
But, for good and/or ill,
  sexual norms can no longer be imposed
  by an appeal to power,
unless there is an alliance
  with the punitive power of the state,
Elsewhere there is no alternative
  to advancing moral convictions
  other than by persuasion,
  seeking people's free consent.
In practice, ethical judgments are usually made
  in the context of pastoral care
  rather than of authoritative pronouncements.
Theologically informed ethical thinking
  is now only advisory.

A bit of pondering on religion and authority.

The Latin root of the word 'religion' is 're-ligare'.
  It is thought that the image in mind
    is that of a bundle of sticks tied together.

In the life of the Roman Empire this implied that
  religion was about 'binding',
  but it was interpreted as
    being tied back,
    being tied to the past,
    almost, to be cemented into the foundation.

So to be in a position of authority in religion
  meant being responsible for
    binding every action to the sacred beginning,
    bearing the whole weight of the past,
    indeed possessing 'gravitas',
    the ability to bear the weight.

So there was a constant looking to the past,
and authority was exercised
  externally and impersonally,
characteristically by resort to
  the letter of the law, force, and punishment.

Ask in what ways that notion of religion and authority
  still informs the practice of the churches
  and of society today.

And your own practice.

I too am inclined to have my scapegoat of the month.
If I were a dictator, my first action would be to ...

Now think of the roots of 'authority'
  in the words 'author'
  and 'augment'.
Authority comes from being in touch with the origins,
  but not bound to the past in a rigid external way.
Change and growth are possible,
  and authority's aim is to help them happen
  in as creative way as the original founding act.
This use of authority works itself out in
  sustaining others
    and enabling them to flourish,
  in upholding others
    and not denying them a place,
  in always being alert
    to the particulars of circumstances.
The binding is now for the purposes of the common good,
  not simply to precedent.
Authority makes itself felt in a liberating way
  when we converse together
    to unfold the meaning of
    tradition then and experience now,
  in places where people feel secure enough
    to tell it as it is.
But it is naive to suppose that authority
  can always be exercised in this way.
It is sentimental to suppose
  that everybody can be welcomed all the time.
The authority has to be invested in some 'body',
    (whether a person or a group),
  with limited powers for a limited time,
    accountable to the wider community,
  that can take emergency action,
  to stop traffic when the emergency services
    are rushing to rescue people who are trapped,
  to stop bullies who will otherwise
    impose an authoritarian regime
    and ride roughshod over the vulnerable.

Bishop	Yes, well, that all seems satisfactory.
	There's just one other issue.
	Er ... er ...
	Can I put it this way?
	I would want to know if you had a partner
	and wanted him to share the vicarage,
	and I would want you to offer to resign.
Interviewee	Yes, I see. I think I understand.
	But can I clarify this a little?
	Presumably there is no problem
	if I want to have a lodger.
Bishop	(laughing) No, of course not.
Interviewee	Right. Now suppose that a family
	had nowhere to live for a few months
	and I took them into the vicarage,
	and because of space
	the lodger and I had to share a bedroom.
	Would that cause you any problems?
Bishop	(with a nervous twitch)
	Well - er - no.
Interviewee	And because we didn't want to spend
	any money on temporary furniture,
	if the lodger and I had to share a bed,
	would that in itself
	be a reason for resignation?
Bishop	(gyrating uncomfortably in armchair)
	Er - no.

Interviewee refrained from knife-twisting. A subsequent letter from the bishop asked that he be informed about any partner and that the circumstances be discussed ...

An American cartoon showed two men
   with arms round each other
   talking to a bishop at a cocktail party.

One of them says,

'Well, bishop, it was a choice
   between homosexuality and ordination,
   and I took the more spiritual option.'

A few statements about sex from repentant bishops?

1   We inherit a tradition which has often said
          that sex is unfortunate if not bad,
          and pleasure is suspect.
       This has not helped.

2   Like everyone else,
          we have gut reactions of disgust,
          we are repelled and offended by instinct.
       This has not helped.

3   In the early days of our ministry
          some of us conducted a service
          for the 'purification of women after childbirth',
          as though they could not be admitted back
          into the community until they had been cleansed.
       This has not helped.

4   Some of us have memories of schooldays
          and of activity in dormitories
          which have left us with mixed emotional memories
          of pleasure and guilt, disgust and fascination,
          and makes it hard for us to think
          that some men choose to live together -
          let alone women.
       This has not helped.

5   We wear sexually ambivalent robes
          and signal by dog collars
          that everything below the neck is irrelevant.
       One of our best loved prayers,
          'God be in my head',
          gets as far down as the heart,
          but no further.
       This has not helped.

Statements from bishops about lesbian and gay clergy?...

1   We know you exist,
        and find it tiresome that you won't go away.
        Why can't you keep everything hidden
        so that we don't have to talk about it?

2   Publicly we insist you be sexually abstinent.
      Privately, some of us ask you to be discreet.

3   Keep knowledge of your sexual orientation private,
      and, if at all possible, completely secret.

4   Pretend you are a heterosexual bachelor
      (this from those who also usually act in the mode
        of hierarchical and military male authority).

5   Find others of like mind for discreet support
      (this from those who are often the most uneasy
        about the ordination of women,
        and frequently belong to misogynist cliques,
        and among whom a penchant for lace and gold
        is not unknown).

6   Whatever you do,
        don't *flaunt* your sexuality.

NB

      Not all of us are negative.
      A few of us have other things to say.
          (See next page)

      And to statement 6,
      Oh yes, and what about all that brocade and silk?
      Also, 'flaunt' is a weasel word which hides
        an anger about people who disturb us
        by refusing to let us get away with ignoring them.

Heard from a few bishops to lesbian and gay clergy:

- Work in an inner-city parish among those
    who know what it is like to be oppressed.
  Be as openly gay as you can without its politics
    totally consuming your ministry,
  and struggle for justice alongside
    the ethnic minority, the unemployed,
    the single parents.

- Be as openly gay as you can:
    your honesty will be respected
    by those who really matter;
  women who have been abused will find you safe;
  and your anger and sense of humour
    will bring zest to the life of the parish.

- Secrecy leads to
    hypocrisy,
    frustration,
    lies,
    fear,
  a deadening of faith,
  a loss of enthusiasm for life,
  and an embittering of spirit.
  We want none of it for ourselves or for you.

- We want you to be self-affirming,
  (as we would wish women and black people to be),
  not self-confessed
  (which makes you sound like thieves).

[part of a sequence, pp. 229-239]

- We now know that homosexuality is
    about relationships and love
and that it is therefore much more than being
    about the one act that obsessed so many of us.

'Bugger' comes from the Latin 'bulgarius',
    i.e. Bulgarian, also regarded in the Middle Ages as
    a heretic and a usurer.
We do not wish to scapegoat
the few Seventh Day Adventist
    Eastern European
    bankers of our acquaintance.

'Sodomy' is a word derived from the biblical
    story of Sodom and Gomorrah.
Nobody is absolutely sure what the crime of
    the men of Sodom was,
but we would agree that
    the threatened rape was (and remains) an offence
    against the code of hospitality to strangers
    and against the law of love.
And we will no longer use the word.

[part of a sequence, pp 229-239]

- Repression of homosexual feelings
    has been characteristic of men
    with military and political power
    in European societies,
a repression which led them to load
    their guilt and self-hatred
    on to those men
    who were obviously or openly gay,
and totally to ignore lesbian women.
They have consistently supported
    punitive measures against
    various sexual (and also racial) groups.
Many bishops have been part of this repression.
But we do not wish to be associated any longer
    with that structure of thought and practice.

[part of a sequence, pp. 229-239]

• Those who are heterosexual among us
  have been comfortable with the experience of
  making love privately with our spouses
  on Saturday night
and presiding at the Eucharist publicly
  on Sunday morning.
We have not felt that we needed cleansing
  from an impure and polluted act
before we joined with our fellow Christians
  in celebrating the love God makes with us.
Making love sexually is the best way of preparing to
  make love spiritually:
actually there is little difference between the two,
  and this may be the reason that
  people who are enjoying a full sexual life
  are not often in church on Sunday mornings.
So we claim that there is no *reason*
  to be offended by the knowledge
  that a vicar who is gay or lesbian
  has slept with his or her partner
  on a Saturday night
  (nor, let it also be said)
  that a vicar at the altar is pregnant).

[part of a sequence, pp 229-239]

- We have realized that to scapegoat someone
     or some category of persons
     is to treat them as less than fully human.
  In the past we have thought that women
     were less fully formed than men,
  that Jews were less human than Christians,
  and that homosexual people too were subhuman.
  Against this we affirm the neglected tradition
     of loving the ones our darkened minds wish
        to label as our enemies,
     not least the enemy within,
     those feelings of sexual fear, guilt, and shame
     that we could not cope with,
     repressed from memory,
     and projected on to the vulnerable.
  We have heeded the warning that Primo Levi gave:

  'Many people - many nations -
     can find themselves holding,
     more or less wittingly,
     that "every stranger is an enemy".
  For the most part the conviction lies deep down
     like some latent infection;
  it betrays itself only in random, disconnected acts,
     and does not lie at the base of a system of reason.
  But when this does come about,
     when the unspoken dogma becomes
     the major premise in a syllogism,
     then, at the end of the chain,
     is the concentration camp.
  Here is the product of a conception of the world
     carried rigorously to its logical conclusion;
  so long as the conception subsists,
     the conclusion remains to threaten us.
  The story of the death camps should be understood
     by everyone as a sinister alarm-signal.'

[part of a sequence, pp. 229-239]

Source: Primo Levi, *If This is a Man*, Bodley Head, 1960, from the preface, with acknowledgment

- We now admit that our own conception
    of what we called homosexuality,
    what we saw, our actual perception,
    was limited and distorted,
  and we refused to see
    because we did not want to face up
    to the implications of change.
  We did not see that our collusion
    with blinkered assumptions led us
    to speak with patronizing slogans
    and self-righteous rhetoric.
  Thus we made life more difficult
    for the confused, the uncertain, the vulnerable.
  We would wish to honour those who stood up
    and refused to collude with our scapegoating,
    who refused to consent to our interpretations,
    and who gently and firmly and openly
    claimed their place in the sun.
  Many of them were hurt,
    and we have reaped the benefit of their sacrifice.
    We salute them.

[part of a sequence, pp 229-239]

•   It has been a difficult journey, full of pitfalls.
Our refusal to allow our troubled darkness
    to come into the light made us exclude people
        from membership and ministry,
an exclusion that was backed by unjust laws.
Those who stood up and were counted had to face
    the reality that the excluders had more power.
We ourselves were among the powerful excluders.
We remember with penitence that
    Jesus refused the power that dominates
    and used the power that liberates,
and that he identified himself with the excluded.
It was not that he *wanted* to be a victim,
    but that he realized that
    the message and practice of inclusion
    would have dire personal consequences.
But in keeping his heart open to the powerful,
    being willing to forgive them their blindness,
    he drew the sting of their attack,
    ultimately allowing them no power over him.
He brought the dark game
    of dominance and submission,
    of self-righteousness and scapegoating,
    of our fears of sexuality and aggression,
    into the light,
so that the dynamic might become so clear to us
    that we would no longer need to repeat it.
It is taking us a long time to learn this lesson.

[part of a sequence, pp. 229-239]

• It is never easy to change hearts,
    our own or other people's.
It is never easy to risk shaming the powerful
    or to be on the receiving end of such shaming.
We have not learned how to do completely without
    the sanction of coercion.
But we have become alert to the need
    for changes in the law of the land
    and for changes in church policy,
so that where hearts have not yet been warmed
    and eyes not yet opened,
the law can
    restrain the worst excesses of power,
    protect the weak and the vulnerable,
    and guard legitimate privacies.
Good laws about sexual activity
    are like good laws about national parks -
they protect a vulnerable landscape
    while enabling people's enjoyment of it.
And even good laws cannot guarantee
    that people will act with wisdom,
    appreciating the need for boundaries,
    and gladly putting them into place themselves.

[part of a sequence, pp. 229-239]

- From time to time we have to bring in force of law.
  If a vicar's behaviour renders his or her ministry
    impossible or ineffective,
  if that behaviour is inordinate,
    so that the ministry of leadership
    in a particular place lacks all credibility,
  there has to be some means
    of withdrawing authority to minister.
  We have, however, learned something
    more than a curt dismissal.
  We always include a number of people
    in an ongoing process of review,
  so that in a crisis they can be called upon
    to help discern the wisest course.
  Even rough justice demands
    as much participation in the process
    by those most directly affected,
  and there must always be
    arbitration and appeal in the background.
  It is patronizing, to say the least,
    that we will lose a night's sleep
    if a person's livelihood is at stake.
  So we try to work with that person over the months
    to discern a more fulfilling Yes
    to what will be a future different from the past,
    and into which the present No
    can be taken up and transformed.
  It seems to us that judgment is creative
    only if there is a vision before us
    of something more attractive and compelling,
    more demanding and satisfying,
    than the one we currently perceive.
  It was that kind of vision by which
    lesbian and gay people creatively judged us.
  (We also wish to act in this way over matters of
    clerical arrogance, pastoral incompetence, and
    collusion with greed.)

[part of a sequence, pp. 229-239]

- We are on a moving train.
  Sometimes we have to move to the back
    and ease hands off the brakes.
  Sometimes we have to move to the front
    and ease hands off the accelerator.
  We do not wish the train to come apart
    in the middle:
  the front half would leap ahead and crash;
  the rear half would grind to a halt.
  We may sometimes seem too hasty to some,
    and too cautious to others.
  But we do recognize that we have to keep moving.
  We are in a different landscape
    from that of our ancestors,
  even though we are on the same train.

  We wish to be loyal to our inheritance
    and consolidate the best of the past.
  We wish to be resilient and full of humour
    as we keep the conflicts open and moving,
    and hold together those who are at odds.
  We want to give the future room to breathe.
  We encourage the vocal minorities.
    We need you to go against the grain;
    we are mature enough to ask you to show us
    how we should all change.
    Without you we should become fossils.
  We wish with you to commend the God of the Jesus
    who did not know how not to love.

[part of a sequence, pp. 229-239]

- We associate ourselves, even if late in the day,
    with what some of us said in 1979,
  then a dissenting minority of bishops
    in the American Episcopal Church:

  'We are ... deeply conscious of, and grateful for,
    the profoundly valuable ministries
      of ordained persons,
    known to us to be homosexual,
    formerly and presently engaged
    in the service of this Church.
  Not all of these persons
    have necessarily been celibate;
  and in the relationships of many of them,
    sustained in the face of social hostility
    and against great odds,
  we have seen a redeeming quality
    which in its way and according to its mode
    is no less a sign to the world of God's love
    than is the more usual sign of Christian marriage.
  From such relationships
    we cannot believe God to be absent.
  Furthermore, even in cases
    where an ideally stable relationship has not,
    or has not yet, been achieved,
  we are conscious of ordained homosexual persons
    who are wrestling responsibly,
    and in the fear of God,
    with the Christian implications of their sexuality,
  and who seek to be responsible, caring,
    and non-exploitative people
  even in the occasionally more transient relationships
  which the hostility of our society towards homosexual
    persons -
  with its concomitants of furtiveness and clandestinity -
    makes inevitable.'

[part of a sequence, pp. 229-239]

There is an argument that
   something acceptable for lay people isn't for clergy.
(That something might be
   the re-marriage of divorced persons
   or a homosexual relationship.)
Is this a matter of higher standards,
   or double standards,
   or one standard more consistently lived up to?
To make the distinction may be a liberal tactic
   for softening the process of institutional change.
But embedded in the comparison is the assumption
   that it would be better not to be married again,
   or not to have a same-sex relationship at all.
The implication is that such couples in congregations
   are second-class citizens.
But the only 'ideal', the only 'high standard' is love,
   the intimacies of affection, sex, trust and loyalty,
   the justice of consistent goodwill and action
     towards the well-being of the whole community.
We all fall short of that 'ideal'.
And who are we to judge
   any group of people of sincere intent
   as more or less 'ideal' than we?
Unless same-sex relationships
   are intrinsically and unequivocally bad,
   there must be some good in them.
(Who will judge what is good enough?)
If so, they are as appropriate for clergy as for laity.
Because the powers that be do not often
   stand with those who live daily with discrimination
   and are not known to enjoy their company,
they will be experienced
   as standing against those struggling for change,
   as refusing to listen,
   and therefore as having no authority
     beyond the coercive,
   none that is authentic through having been earned.

Institutions, especially religious ones,
  go through four stages
  when challenged to change the rule book:

1   They deny there is a problem.
      They lift the corner of the ecclesiastical carpet
        when they hope nobody is looking,
      and sweep the offending 'dirt' underneath -
        where of course it festers,
          and even begins to stink.

2   They admit there is a challenge,
        but argue vociferously against any change.
      This stage has the virtue of clearing the air.
      Movements for change begin,
        both inside and outside the institution.

3   They make exceptions to the old rules.
      Under certain circumstances, for example,
      married priests may be acceptable;
      a second marriage may be permitted
        (for the laity of course, but not for the clergy);
      gay and lesbian couples may be welcomed
        as communicant members of congregations
      (especially if the short-sighted are convinced
        they are two brothers or two sisters).

4   They reinterpret the Tradition,
      and claim that what appears to be a new rule
      is actually a more refined interpretation of the old.
      This is the face-saver
        and keeps people of different opinion together.
      Synods make solemn pronouncements.
      Continuity and connection are preserved.

There were only two new seminarians
   in the Roman Catholic Church in Ireland in 1997.
Is this because the majority of priests are gay,
   and young men looking at the Church
   no longer either need or want a haven
   that is at one level safe
   and at another dehumanizing?
There is no need any more
   to run away from one's sexuality.

Actually, the more important reason
   may be that we have seen through the ecclesiastical game
   of controlling people through guilt and fear
   in the name of a god of terror.
And the institutions and governance of the Church
   continue to be ill-suited to embodying a God of Love.

Church authorities are uneasy
　　about licensing clergy to work
　　among gay and lesbian people.

Are pastors called to account when they minister to
　　(to their souls of course)
arms traders,
drug traffickers,
land grabbers,
dictators and their secret police,
ethnic 'cleansers',
biological weapon manufacturers,
mind controllers,
political brainwashers
　　(and their ecclesiastical equivalents,
　　from the likes of Opus Dei
　　to authoritarian leaders and evangelists)

let alone their silent colluders
　　(the rest of us)?

'Mother' Church
    finds it difficult to relate
    to grown-up men and women.

She may dismiss even the possibility of women being
    ordained,
or she may grudgingly allow them as long as they model
    themselves on the men.
(Woman's animus on the loose is an unpleasant thing.)

She does not allow her clergymen to be sexual,
    spiritual and intellectual yes,
    but spirited and embodied no.
If she really delights in their sexuality,
    she will lose her power over them,
    and no longer be able to emasculate them.

But the women of our day are on the move,
    some at ease with both anima and animus within,
    some working with men at ease with both.
Men are less content to be mother church's toy boys -
    or even stipend boys (better not call it rent).
They will no longer perform one night stands at the altar,
    with a ritual divorced from the language and concerns
        of men and women today,
    and consequently and disastrously
        out of touch with the 'communion',
        even no longer 'in communion'.
For communion to be holy,
    it must be an act of love
    of men and women together
    and together in God.

A resolution of the Lambeth Conference
   of the bishops of the Anglican Communion in 1998
acknowledged that lesbian and gay people
   were full members of the Church,
   and should be listened to carefully,
while making it clear that
      they should not have sexual relationships;
      they could not have a relationship openly blessed;
      they could not be ordained unless celibate.

The attempt to be caring towards individuals
   obscured the difficulty of addressing issues of justice.
Those who are strong on personal compassion
   but weak on structures and policies
come across as patronising to individuals
   and unable to work through anger and conflict.

The listening does not take place on level ground:
lesbian and gay people have heard
   relentless repeats of old scripts,
and those who voted to listen
   had actually refused to do so at the conference itself.
Also those whose relationships and livelihoods
   are at risk,
and those who have learned how to be silent
   and so are not at ease in talking about themselves,
are unlikely to make their voices heard
   as easily as those who are professionally articulate
   and have their hands on the levers of power.

[part of a sequence, pp. 245-248]

It seems that there was an alliance, however informal,
  between hardliners,
that is, those who like clear edges, hard lines,
  and who find variety and ambiguity difficult to live with,
  who want the comfort of certainties
  rather than the discomfort of insecurity:

conservative evangelical bishops from the United States,
  with considerable financial resources;

bishops faced with the harder edges of Islam,
  expecting that a positive line on gay and lesbian issues
  would be used as a stick to beat Christians with,

and bishops particularly concerned with relationships
  with the Roman Catholic Church,
  and aware that the Vatican had communicated
  that anything but a hard line
  would make closer union much more difficult to achieve.

Did conformity come before truth?
Did fear of being laughed at and mocked
  come before solidarity with the marginalized?
Did the zealous demand sacrifices of others
  rather than show courage themselves?
Who paid the price for a show of unity
  and the relief that the Anglican Communion
  did not split apart?

[part of a sequence, pp. 245-248]

The debate on sexuality at the Lambeth Conference in 1998 produced these reflections:

1 The mention of homosexuality produces a frenzied reaction in those who do not so react to anything else.

2 Moderate voices were intimidated by hissing from fellow bishops.

3 A journalist, Andrew Brown, felt an atmosphere of the lynch mob, a 'miasma of poisonous despair'.

4 One of the bishops, Peter Selby, felt the atmosphere sinister, like that of the Nuremberg Rally.

5 To pillory lesbian and gay people is an easy way of demonstrating a hatred of all things liberal.

6 Many bishops demonstrated their *hatred* of lesbian and gay people by the very fact of loud and vigorous condemnation.

7 The celebration of unity at the end of the Conference was at the *expense* of the *expendables*.

[part of a sequence, pp. 245-248]

We need to be careful about large gatherings:

1   where few understand the dynamics of such occasions;

2   where participants are used to dealing with conflicts in a personal and pastoral mode with insight, but in a corporate and institutional mode with ignorance;

3   where there are no structures of constitution and accountability;

4   therefore, where emotional reaction and strong feelings can sweep through and dominate decision-taking - and such undercurrents are always present, powerful even when not visible;

5   where, with a three-minute time limit on speeches, you can hurl scriptural quotations but hardly produce a reasoned argument.

[part of a sequence, pp. 245-248]

10
ENGAGING IN DIALOGUE

I remember chasing a mythical beast,
  the hermeneut.
It was a way of poking fun at theological jargon,
  at the discipline of 'hermeneutics',
  the theory of how we understand.

But I learn this from it
  as I wrestle with others of different convictions:

1 Respect the *otherness* of the other,
    or you will be a prey to manipulation.

2 Listen to the other with open-mindedness,
    whether to person or text or tradition or context.

3 Search for the real questions, the deepest ones.
    Proceed by question and answer, and by dialogue.

4 Declare your interests,
    especially your vested interests,
    for they are often a bar to understanding
    and to liberation.
    Self-deception is characteristic of *all*.

5 Be suspicious.

6 Be rigorous.

7 Never expect to have the last word.
    Keep on seeking insight, reflecting, discerning.

Twelve straight steps:

1. Why do you have to flaunt it?

2. I'm not like you at all.

3. I'm afraid of you.

4. OK, yes, you grew up in a family too.

5. Ah, yes, I wouldn't want to say my fiancé(e) is my lodger.

6. I hadn't thought of that before.

7. I want to listen and learn.

8. Tell me how I've hurt you.

9. I've not always treated those closest to me as kindly and justly as I should have done.

10. I enjoy your company - even if I'm a bit afraid my reputation will suffer.

11. I'll march with you.

12. I laugh with you.

Churches have difficulties with lesbian and gay issues:

1 They are used to pronouncements from on high
   that are to be obeyed
   or to debate in which only one side wins;
   they are not used to dialogue
   in which all parties are open to being changed.

2 They tend to think that all necessary truth
   has already been given.
   They do not use the past to find examples
   of people who in faith launch into the future.

3 They tend to feel embattled in what they perceive
   as an uncomprehending and hostile society,
   and are not used to the idea
   that God is at work everywhere.

4 They value those who speak familiar words
   and suspect the disturbers on the edge.

5 Their clergy guard the flock
   and monitor and censor resources,
   rather than provide the range of resources
   and help people discern the truth
   and make their own moral decisions.

6 They are uneasy about letting controversial groups
   use church premises and facilities,
   and think that honest engagement
   will compromise them.

Source: Michael Vasey, *Strangers and Friends*, Hodder and Stoughton, 1995, with acknowledgment.

Most church statements about homosexuality
  are either uncompromisingly negative
  or uncomfortably constipated.
The authors
  wriggle with distaste,
  distance themselves with ideals,
  and reluctantly concede an exception or two.
There is little to show
  for such an agonizing squeeze.
It is at best theology above the neck,
  with only a rare theologian
  showing he or she knows what it is
  to be embodied and passionate.
That is an emotional (I hope not irrational) response
  to reading the St Andrew's Day Statement
  and some parts of a subsequent book of commentaries.
But the subtitle put me off:
  Christian Voices on Homosexuality and the Church -
  it made me feel once again that I was being dissected.
I wonder why only one of the original signatories and only
  one of the subsequent contributors to the book is a
  woman (one in seven, and one in thirteen).
Also, the Statement's theological convictions are expressed
  in language that feels disconnected from people.
Nor do they give any indication that all such statements
  are provisional,
or that much of what has been inherited and presented as
  'orthodox' would exclude those who wish to give such
  creeds considered and considerable scrutiny.
That has little to do with lesbian and gay people as such,
  but has everything to do with how theology is barren
  when detached from their experience and witness.

Source: Timothy Bradshaw (ed.), *The Way Forward, Christian Voices on
Homosexuality and the Church*, Hodder and Stoughton, 1997 reproduced by
permission of the publishers. My reaction was not negative to all the
contributors, and the good thing about the book is its willingness to
incorporate very different approaches as a contribution to the ongoing debate.

What might it mean for a gay man to be 'healed'?

His personality slowly maturing as he engages
  in the delights and difficulties of an intimate
  and committed relationship with another man? *Or*

The re-alignment of his sexual orientation through
  healing the emotional breach with his father
  by being intimate but not sexual with another man,
  and once that bonding has been achieved,
  becoming open to the possibility of a heterosexual
    relationship?
(This is the approach of evangelical 'counselling'
    agencies,
  backed by the psychological theories of Elizabeth Moberly,
  and the assumption that everyone is born heterosexual
  and that anyone with homosexual feelings
  would not wish anybody else to know about it.) *Or*

Collusion with society's ideal of masculinity
  and its continuing hostility to gay men,
thus achieving a *sense* of healing
  because now at ease with the dominant culture,
but at the expense of his own sensitivities
  and a continuing attitude of exclusion towards
    openly gay men?
(This is a kind of 'cure' by emotional amputation:
  survival with a perhaps unnecessary limp.) *Or*

An inner integration which comes from
  confronting hostility and its underlying idolatry,
  (which glories in macho masculinity as its god)
  and pursuing an alternative vision of society,
  one of whose welcome variants is
  the self-affirming and self-confident gay man?

Source: Michael Vasey, *Strangers and Friends*, Hodder and Stoughton, 1995, with acknowledgment.

Who is responsible for the existence of gay ghettoes?

Think of a gay teenager growing up
   in rural Nevada or Galloway,
   or small-town Louisiana or Cornwall.
90% of the messages received about homosexuality
   will have been hostile,
   from local press to schools, homes to churches.
He or she will take the first opportunity to move away,
   drawn to where there is a degree of openness,
   to San Francisco or Glasgow, to New York or London,
   to discover a safe place
   in which to find a name, an identity, and friends.

If the editors and teachers and parents and ministers
   had given a positive, relaxed, and inclusive message
   that lesbian and gay people are valued in the community
   and in their extended families,
most of them would have wished to meet
   only in ways similar to those who share any concern -
   from Amnesty International to local churches:
     for mutual support,
     for education and mission,
     for celebration.

William Swing, Episcopal Bishop of California wrote:
   'We have a homosexual ghetto as a monument
   to families all over the United States of America
   who cannot deal with their homosexual children.'

A report which included estimates of the incidence
  of homosexual behaviour in Britain
claimed a range of 6.1% to 1.1% of men
  and a range of 3.4% to 0.4% of women.
Even if you take the lowest estimate for men
  you have a figure of 570,000,
which is slightly larger than the Jewish population
  and slightly smaller than the Methodist population.
Arguments about what is lawful and just
  should not depend on how large and small
  a particular population may be,
  but on what is lawful and just.

Nobody of course knows
  what the lesbian and gay population is.
When there is no longer any reason to be afraid,
  those who conduct surveys will not be lied to,
  and some of those who *say*
    they are exclusively heterosexual in behaviour
  may find they do not have to pretend any more.

Source: The National Survey of Sexual Attitudes and Lifestyles, 1994

'Most researchers now believe that adult sexual orientation
   is usually established before the age of puberty
   in both boys and girls ...
The purpose of age of consent legislation
   is to protect vulnerable young people
   from sexual exploitation and abuse,
but there is no clear justification
   for a differential age for homosexual male activity
   and other sexual activity.
Unwelcome sexual attentions
   of a seriousness warranting criminal prosecution
   are equally offensive
   whether the victim is a man or a woman:
   the same law should apply to all.'

'More than 50% of homosexual and bisexual men
   had their first homosexual experience by age 16
   and over 90% by age 18.
74% reported that they had suspected
   that they were "sexually different"
and 67% had labelled themselves as "homosexual or gay"
   before they first had sex with another man.
60% of first homosexual encounters
   were with a partner within two years of their own age
   and most were hoped for or actively sought.'

So there is no evidence that younger men are 'seduced'
   into a way of life that they do not really want.
There is every evidence that the criminal law
   does not act as a deterrent.
Most young gay men are aware of their orientation
   before they are 16
and they seek partners of their own age.

Sources: British Medical Association; Sigma Project financed by the
Department of Health and the Medical Research Council

Fundamentalist sects
   and the Roman Catholic Church
have one thing in common:
   they both claim the possession of absolute truth
   and infallible guides,
whether they be the Scriptures, the teaching of the Church,
   or the Pope.
They believe that what they have to say
   has direct relevance, in their own terms,
   to the whole of humankind.
They attempt to convert others,
   and while the rest of the world remains unconverted,
   they operate from fortresses with high walls,
   making crusades into a hostile world.

But they have lost control of the terms and contents
   of the human agenda,
and in the foreseeable future
   there seems no chance of their retrieving it.

More and more of the people we have contact with
   are different from ourselves,
whether by ethnic background, religious conviction,
   cultural custom, or sexual orientation,
with media and internet readily available
   and constantly intrusive.
Even the children of Jehovah's Witnesses
   educated at home cannot escape such influences for long.

A pluralistic world is beginning to shape values
   that may be influenced by religious groups,
   but cannot be expressed in religious terms
   if they are to be accepted by everybody.
We use the language of rights - and of responsibilities -
   but not of specific beliefs.
We use the processes of dialogue and conflict resolution,
   engaging with differences in hope.

The influence of the free market:

1 The *real* world is one of male competition,
    with the virtues of self-reliance
        and emotional restraint.
    This is so both at work and in sports.
    Male bonding is real,
        but with the goal of improving competitiveness.
    Too much intimacy is deemed a weakness,
        there is a limit to demonstrations of affection,
        and sexual desire is relegated to the secretive.

2 Religion becomes a matter of personal choice,
        and churches become voluntary associations,
        largely detached from major public concerns.

3 Affection, desire, love and friendship
        become at least semi-privatized
        and focused for most people on the home.

4 Space can be created for subcultures
        and for niche markets,
    either of which can be substantial
        in size and influence.

5 The former social bonding of friendship
        and of intermarriage dissolves,
    leaving only those of home, voluntary association,
        and commercial alliance,
    the lifespan of any one of which may well be
        much shorter than it used to be.

Source: Michael Vasey, *Strangers and Friends*, Hodder and Stoughton, 1995, p. 847, with acknowledgment.

The influence of science and technology:

1   Information, order, and control
        become highly valued.
    The sphere of the personal can be sidelined.

2   Its spotlight on sexual matters included
        examining 'homosexuality' as a behavioural phenomenon.
    The word itself was coined as a medical term in 1869.

3   It became customary to categorize people,
        with a particular emphasis on
        the criminal and the deviant -
    and the statistically deviant
        were often (unscientifically) regarded as
        morally deviant.

4   Crime and sickness were the usual categories
        into which homosexual behaviour was classified,
        with some shift from the first to the second.
    (As sin, it remains so classified by the churches,
        but their influence is in decline.)
    The shift was significant in debates in the sixties
        about changing the law on homosexual acts:
    what was a crime came to be regarded as a sickness.

5   It was assumed that heterosexual desire
        is natural and that homosexual desire is warped:
    scientific methods were researched in order
        that such desire might be re-directed.
    Few people took seriously the actual existence
        of homosexual *relationships*.

Source: Michael Vasey, *Strangers and Friends*, Hodder and Stoughton, 1995, with acknowledgment.

Know what you may find yourself struggling against
   when faced with fundamentalists.
These elements of their experience are common:
Pressure is put on the individual by a pastor
   or by a group,
sometimes with intense prayer,
sometimes with literal wrestling,
   as if to drive out the demon of homosexuality.
This is not very different from aversion therapy,
   what was referred to as a 'corrective method'.
Note the language and atmosphere of punishment
   and force.
'I confess to you (or to this house church)
   that I have homosexual feelings.
Help me, Jesus, I a sinner,
   worthless and degenerate,
   tempted to indulge in wicked acts.
I give myself to you.'
Experiencing acceptance by the group
   and finding release through being open,
   there is a surge of relief and joy,
   and a sincere belief in having been saved by Jesus.
'Thank you, Jesus, for converting me,
   and delivering me from my sin.'
Some months later homosexual feelings return.
'I've been converted.
I don't know what's got into me.
It can't really be me that's doing these things.
It must be the Devil.
And the Devil's agents are all around.
I must attack all gay people with zeal.'
Or the distress is internalized.
'I've been tempted and I've fallen.
   I am in despair: better to take my own life
   than to degrade myself further and corrupt others.'
The suicide note.

Another myth is that gay men
    are out to convert others to their way of life.

It's like a contagion,
    and it spreads like a prairie fire.

Huh?
    Show me the smoke.

And as for conversion -
    if you want to use that language -
the conversion rate of heterosexual people
    must be appallingly low
and the lapses phenomenally high.

It's not as if being lesbian or gay
    were one endless round of ease, joy, and pleasure -
though I suspect that is another myth
    in the minds of the hard-working and dutiful.

Think about it:
    It will be great to be bullied in the school grounds.
    It will be wonderful to be called names and insulted.
    It will be easy to walk in and out of a gay pub.

Maybe not in much of London or Manchester,
    but in Truro, Barrow, Pontypool, or Inverness?

The existence of human beings
   whose primary sexual and emotional attraction
   is towards those of their own gender
seems to be a fact of life
   in every society and civilization known to us.

What those human beings *do* about that fact,
   both the minority themselves
   and the rest of the community,
is more varied,
   often particular to one place or period.
The responses are not uniform,
   rather bewilderingly complex.

Some people focus on the universal fact,
   and look at how *individuals* respond to
   and are treated by the wider community,
   whose norms are taken for granted.
Individuals may have to change
   to be assimilated,
   to become as much like everyone else as possible.

Others focus on the *community*,
   and ask how all the members of a society
   can work together on structures and attitudes,
   and expect that in the process the norms will change.

When I speak,
  I use my lips and tongue and vocal cords.
When I write,
  I use my fingers.
These physical acts
  can be *distinguished* from the words I write or speak
  but cannot be *separated* from them.
Further,
  it is *I as a person*
  who am responsible for *the words I write or speak*.

Similarly,
  you can *distinguish* between sexual acts
  and the person who performs them,
  but you cannot *separate* the two.
When I write, when I make love,
  I am getting in touch
  by an act of communication/communion
  with others/another.

I am different from you.
We are not 'all the same underneath'.
But you are not so different from me
   that I should treat you in a different way
   from the way in which I hope you will treat me.
I may not be able to be separate from you,
   as an isolated individual,
but I am different from you,
   I am singular,
and you are singular -
   where singular is not opposite to plural,
   but opposite to grey and boring.
What those who believe themselves to be 'in Christ'
   would want to say is
not that all differences are abolished,
   but that all unjust structures and attitudes are overcome.
To be 'in Christ'
   is to acknowledge and act upon the reality
   that because we belong together for ever in God,
   then maleness and femaleness are significant
   only for variety, diversity, singularity,
   and not for status, superiority, exclusion.

An argument between two Christian men,
  one putting the case for change.
  the other putting the case for the status quo.

The logic of the one is to do his best to make sure
  the other has no power in the institutional Church,
  and will try to get him outvoted in any synod election.
The logic of the other is to get the first excommunicated.

The first has to take care that the other does not try
  to paper over the differences between them
  by smiling and saying that he doesn't think there is much
    that separates them.
The differences are profound.

The first may want to ask the second whether or not
  he is thoroughly literalist in his reading of the Bible.
He may breathe a sigh of relief when the second
 declines to punish by bringing in the death penalty.
Once this single inconsistency is made clear,
  both may admit that they use other criteria
  in deciding how to interpret a biblical passage.

But each has to recognize the other as an enemy,
  however civilized the debate
  and however temporary the enmity.
Neither will relish continuing the conversation.
But it does not help to *pretend* that the enmity is not real.

Dialogue:
   a living process,
   a way of being together
   that respects diversity
   and resolves conflicts.

To engage in dialogue
   I have to give up two cherished attitudes:
that there will be a final, absolute, last word
   at the end of the process;
that I already have that last word
   and all the others are wrong.
Giving up the first is hard for traditionalists,
giving up the second is hard for liberals,
   whose own bigotries are usually
   not far below the surface.
(Author's note: mea culpa.)

(I have seen the word 'dialogue'
   in some statements by bishops,
   and I think it means,
We must take time and care to explain our decision
   so that it will become perfectly clear to you
   that we are right.
You will see the sense of what we have to say,
   you will fall into line,
   and we can settle down to a quieter life.)

We are invited to bring to a dialogue:
   Deep expression of what we really do feel.
   An honest and open telling of our stories.
   A passion for truth and justice.
   As much knowledge as we can gather.
   Generosity of heart and mind.
   Qualities like compassion and vulnerability -
     and a sense of humour:
     a key moment in the process is when everyone laughs ...

You will find it argued that
    maleness and femaleness are good in themselves
    because they are basic to the biological structure of creation,
    because they were created as such by God
       and are not part of the gonewrongness of life:
therefore, a homosexual orientation,
    like a physical disability,
    is part of the 'fallenness' of life as we know it,
    and homosexual acts set up a 'dissonance' in us.

Rather I would argue that
    maleness and femaleness,
    sexual orientation, disability,
    racial type, economic class,
are all part of what is given,
    they are all in themselves *morally* neutral,
and that we experience the created order
    as a mixture of biology, history, sociology, etc.

It is how we use this complex raw material that matters:
it is in our actions and our relationships that we become
    good or bad.

If your assumption is that there is only one 'natural' sexual
    act,
then anything else you may do,
    and that includes masturbation and oral sex,
    is 'dissonant',
and even if the one 'natural' act is performed without the
    willingness of one of the partners,
the act itself is not 'dissonant'.

You are strange.
You disturb me.
My first reaction
is to push you away,
to run away from you.

'I have been on my guard
not to condemn the unfamiliar.
For it is easy to miss God
at the turn of a civilization.'

Source: David Jones, 'A,a,a, Domine Deus', *The Sleeping Lord*, Faber, 1974, p. 9, reproduced by permission of Faber & Faber.Ltd.

I may hope to persuade you to change your mind.
But if you are like me,
    you won't want me to put you in a pressure cooker,
    let alone in a microwave oven.
And though I may be boiling at times,
    I am sure you don't want to be grilled.
Perhaps we can both jump into a slow cooker.
    We shall certainly be changed,
    but at a pace we can manage,
    and we'll be even tastier as a result
        than we are already.

Various outcomes of disagreements:

I win - you lose.   Victory

I lose - you win.   Defeat

I respect the decision
   of the majority and
   will abide by it.   Submission

I lose - I leave.   Schism

I form the *real* church.   Sect

We agree to differ, but
   we don't engage.   Toleration

We differ but we keep
   working at it.   Tension,
                                     liveable with because of dialogue

We all change our
   perspective, recognizing
   that our different
   convictions about what
   is good can be taken up
   and transformed.   Unity in diversity

Five positions:

1 I reject you and I punish you
      if I have the power to do so.
   This is the fundamentalist.

2 I won't punish you but I don't accept you
      unless you are celibate.
   This is the conservative.

3 I accept you though I think you will always
      fall short of the ideal.
   This is the conservative liberal.

4 I accept you and recognize your relationship
      as legally and qualitatively equivalent to marriage.
   This is the more radical liberal.

5 I question the rules of the game
      that you have only two choices -
      heterosexual marriage or celibacy.
   I want to see friendship accepted
      as the all-encompassing and inclusive norm
      for all relationships.
   This is the radical prophet and revolutionary.

Prejudice -
    pre-judging before you have the facts;
    based on powerful emotion working
        as reaction not as response.

Therefore the prejudiced person
    always resists new information,
    is never moveable by argument.

Change comes from
    relationships with people,
    with hearing their stories.

You cannot argue with a story,
    you can only respond personally.

And that may bring to the fore
    a more powerful emotion -
        love
    than the emotion behind the prejudice -
        fear.

If I pray for you,
   who this evening Bible-bashed me in church,
   or queer-bashed me in the park,
if I pray for you, my enemy,

I discover it to be an act of non-violent resistance
   to the violence in you
   and to the violence in myself.

I refuse to separate myself from you completely.
I hold to the truth of my anger and confusion and trembling.
I pray that my emotion will be channelled
   into confronting you -
or, if we never meet again, confronting those like you -
   to shame you,
   to bring you to repentance,
   to have you at my mercy -
and I pray that my mercy will win.

I hold to another truth,
   by keeping inner contact in prayer,
   I refuse to dismiss you as subhuman,
   or allow you to dismiss me as subhuman,
   so dreadful that either of us no longer deserves to live.
If I did that,
   I would merely have adopted your stance towards me.
You would have won.

It is hard to 'keep in touch'
  with those who refuse to touch you,
  who, zealously, push you away,
  or, cowardly, draw back silently.
Either way, you are left feeling isolated,
  forcibly or gently shunted into a siding,
  forgotten by the successful on the main line
(who may, however, not have noticed
  that the infrastructure they take for granted is in decay.)

Some genuinely try to keep in touch.
  We must love the sinner,
    (they say, perhaps a touch too glibly,)
    however much we hate the sin.
  We will tolerate the fact that you are
  homosexually orientated
    (a linguistic mouthful,
    perhaps a sign of lack of ease,)
  but you mustn't practise.
  If you have done, you must repent.
  If you persist and will not repent, you must go.

As if you can be a General Practitioner
  without hands-on diagnosis
  and daily exercise of your profession.
As if you can be a skilled practitioner of archery
  without your quiver full,
  and regular use of bow and arrow.
If asked if you are a practising homosexual,
  quip in reply,
  No, I'm quite good at it:
  I qualified years ago.

And are you a practising judgmental?

Have you been 'born again'?

It's proving a long gestation and a difficult labour.
Has yours been the same?

Or:

Many times.

Do you accept Jesus as your Lord and Saviour?

Do you accept Jesus as your Servant and Healer?

Do you accept Jesus as your Friend and Brother?

Have you been converted?

New every morning.

Do you believe in the Bible?

No, I believe in God.

To be the object of 'hate the sin and love the sinner'
   is to be at best patronised
   and at worst cruelly used.

Take a different kind of behaviour.
   If you have murdered or raped,
   you would not expect the distinction
     between sin and sinner,
   nor would it be put into practice by others.
The murderer or rapist -
   the *person acting wickedly* - is punished.

Here is a genuinely helpful response:
   I dislike you and I disapprove of what you did.
   There is, however, more to you
     than the murderer that at present
     fills the whole picture I have of you
     and that you have of yourself.
   I will not desert you, I will stand alongside you.
   I believe it is possible
     that I shall one day enjoy your company.
   I believe that my loyalty may make you think -
     and together we may work on the problem:
   How can you change sufficiently
     from the kind of person who harmed another
     to the kind of person who respects others?

That looks a bit pompous in cold print,
   but it may be the credo of a probation officer.

If you try to hate the sin and love the sinner,
   you dangerously separate deed from person,
   and you encourage others separate them.
   This easily leads to blaming an external influence
     for the evil deed.
I don't know what got into me.
     Blame Teddy - or the Devil.

It is a difficult spiritual path.
But it may be the first step in learning
how to love an enemy.

Dare I risk being identified with the outcast
(the neighbours will call it
being tarred with the same brush)?

Dare I bear the ambivalence of love and hate
within myself?

Dare I resist the pressure to distance myself?

Dare I face the challenge of not running away?

Dare I face the other with precisely the same challenge?

Dare I admit and stay with my own brokenness?

Dare I admit that I may be more broken than the other?

Dare I live with the possibility
that I may have to change
more than the one whom I had condemned
as 'more sinful than I'?

Dare we together trust in a Love
that bears the pain of dislocation
until relationships are restored in justice,
but in ways that neither of us can predict,
that bring profound change to both of us?

And if this is true for two people
who may both recognize that wrong has been done,
might it not also be true for two people
whose relationship is strained
because they at present discern differently?

There have always been tensions
  between settlers and nomads,
  between householders and itinerants,
  between traditionalists and pioneers,
  between shrine guardians and iconoclasts.

If we keep on talking,
if we keep in touch,
  traditionalists may discover
    that the roots of tradition
      can put forth new shoots,
    that past mutations
      are characteristic of tradition,
  and pioneers may recognize
    that tender plants need protection,
    that they do not have to be isolated
      from a continuing momentum.
We may both be prevented from self-centredness,
  and move towards each other
    out of our fortresses,
    out of our ghettoes.

In confrontation,
  we each have too much to lose.
In dialogue,
  we all have so much to gain.

Why stay in the Church?

For all its faults -
   and it is made up of mixed up people like me,
   and so I can hardly expect it to be perfect -
it is the place where
   I have glimpsed a vision,
   I have been touched to the quick -
     and touched slowly too, without fear,
   I have heard words and music
     that have made my heart and mind,
     my emotions and imagination, soar,
   I have been drawn into action
     that seeks to incarnate the vision:

a vision of
   a community genuinely inclusive,
     a house of prayer for all peoples;
   unconditional love as the heart of all life,
     divine and human;
   spirituality and faith embodied,
     joined to flesh and blood;
   human beings never being able finally
     to be separated from one another
       or from the divine;
   justice and the common good
     beyond the rough justice of the law court
     and the rampant individualism of my culture.

So I am prepared to stay with and work with
   hostility and tension,
   perplexity and pain,
and to celebrate the occasional firstfruits
   of unity-in-diversity,
   of communion-through-darkness,
   of common weal-beyond-our-devising.

A vignette from a local synod
  (a deanery synod to be precise,
  with only one member under the age of 40)
  in a diocese of the Church of England.
  early in 1998:

Traditional viewpoints
  about homosexual acts and relationships
  were most vividly expressed in three statements:

A woman of mature years who had the courage
  to say what she clearly found embarrassing:
What we're really talking about is buggery.

A member of the pressure group 'Reform'
  commenting on the opinion of the bishops
  in their report on issues of human sexuality
  that lesbian and gay couples
  should be welcomed in congregations:
It is a dose of strychnine in an otherwise good cup of coffee.

An elderly man hobbling out into the winter night
  to one who had argued that welcoming viewpoint:
Have you seen your doctor? I think you should, you know.

When a conservative resolution was put,
  a procedural motion that the synod
    should move to the next item on the agenda
  was *passed* by a majority of two to one.

Human beings need time to work through doubts
  but even the most conservative can change.
Human beings do not like to be railroaded
  into making premature decisions about policies.
Human beings show more kindness and courage
  than their labels - and sometimes their beliefs -
  would lead us to expect.

Zealots
    demand more courage of others
    than of themselves,
    and make other people
    proportionally more vulnerable
    than they themselves are willing to be.

We can all applaud courage
    when we see it.
But we should not force others
    to be courageous.
We should en-courage.

For ourselves,
    we can always find a response
    to the question which is always with us:
What is the next step I need to take,
    what small act of courage
    that will enable me and others to grow?
Such steps are rarely dramatic,
    but like hinges can move heavy doors.
What next step -
    with lover, parent, friend, boss, vicar?
And then the next ...

And we can always look out for ways
    of helping others to work out for themselves
    what their next step of courage should be ...

Of any institution of which you are a part,
  family,
  workplace,
  church,
you need to ask,
  for your own deep well-being,
How polluted is the *atmosphere*
  that I breathe here?

You may be developing a severe
  emotional and spiritual allergy.

You may need to move to a place where,
  as it were,
  the pollen count is not as high.

It may be that there is nowhere to go
  which is not at least mildly poisonous,
  and therefore continually debilitating.

But do ask the question.

Can you avoid the worst places?
Can you take care of your spiritual diet,
  drawing on what really does nourish you?
Can you be alert to the need
  for rapid escape routes in an emergency?

Does this extract from the Diary page of the *Church Times*
by the Rector of Hackney, John Pridmore,
resonate with you?

'"Love bears all things" -
even the Church of England.
Later that same wedding day,
I absented myself from the revels
and slipped into Chichester Cathedral
for the tail-end of Choral Evensong.
I sat at the back of an empty nave.
Far away beyond the screen
someone was reading from the Bible.

"Women should be silent in the churches.
For they are not permitted to speak,
but should be subordinate as the law says.
If there is anything they desire to know,
let them ask their husbands at home.
For it is shameful for a woman to speak in church."

'What would the intelligent young couple
I had just married
have made of that, I wondered?
What must they think of a Church
that continues to authorize the unloading of toxic waste
from its lecterns.
Usually I find such moments comic.
That night I was overwhelmed
by a deep foreboding for my Church.
In that vast deserted house,
for all the aching loveliness of a sublime Nunc Dimittis,
I felt myself as if in the bowels
of some huge abandoned hulk,
drifting towards shipwreck.'

Source: John Pridmore, 'Diary', *Church Times*, 26 February 1999, reproduced
with acknowledgment and thanks.

Michael Vasey was committed
   to evangelical Christianity and to the Church of England
It gradually became known that he was gay,
   and he bravely wrote *Strangers and Friends*
   gently and courteously to help his own constituency
   think more about lesbian and gay people.
It brought him much hostility which may or may not
   have contributed to his death of a heart attack at 51.
Have that in mind as you read this quotation:
'For gay people themselves
   the churches are likely to remain places of danger.
Negotiating life with the church
   will remain difficult for gay people
   who find their love drawn out
   by the mysterious friendship of Jesus Christ.
They ignore at their peril questions of
   spiritual authenticity, personal survival,
   security of employment,
   and the dangers of physical and emotional violence.
They will need safe places in which to learn
   to distinguish the voice of Christ
   from the alien cultural commitments
     of the rest of the church.
They are likely to experience the church of Christ
   as a garden infested with unseen dangers,
   or as a poisoned well.
They will encounter simultaneously
   friendship and betrayal,
   the promise of intimacy and the threat of ostracism.
The water of life will often come mixed
   with a much-prized local vintage
   which gives them little joy or nourishment
   but turns their friends in Christ against them.
They may find themselves, like Jesus,
   suffering "outside the gate".'

Source: Michael Vasey, *Strangers and Friends*, Hodder & Stoughton, 1995, pp. 210-211, with acknowledgment.

Which words do you relish?
  Taste and see.

Queer?	Some use it proudly, others hear too much hatred in it.

Queer?   Some use it proudly,
                    others hear too much hatred in it.

Gay?   Both these words seem too solid
Lesbian?   as nouns, so that the whole person
                       is enveloped by them.
                    Better as adjectives, a quality, a way
                       of describing, a dimension of life.

Homosexual?   From the world of clinical definition,
Heterosexual?   of psychology and medicine. Not too
Bi-sexual?   keen on being dominated by doctors.

Tri-sexual?   Joke. Try anything once ...

Poly-sexual?   Perhaps. I may be attracted quite
                       passionately to a range of people -
                       and even the non-human world.
                    A lover of trees is a dendrophile.

Human sexual?   Yes. And useful in arguments.
                       Reminds me we all belong to one
                       another. But it is also a dodge.

I give up. I think I'm like a real ale produced by
  Theakston's -
an old peculiar,
  distinctive, mature, and full of flavour ...

Until the nineteenth century
   the law referred only to the sexual *acts*
   of buggery or sodomy.

The nineteenth century saw the word 'homosexual'
   for the first time:
it slowly began to be used to refer to people as well as
   to acts,
albeit in terms of sickness.

'Gay' began to spread in the middle of the twentieth
   century partly as a reaction to negative categories,
   summarized as 'pity' at best and 'clobber' at worst.
It was a self-chosen word, not an imposed one.
It indicates a social identity, not simply a personal one.
It clearly includes the specifically sexual,
   but places it in as wide a context as does
   public knowledge of married couples,
   in which relationships sex is presumed to take place,
   and questions of detail are left private.
It shifts power
   from establishments to people,
   from patrons to participants,
   from the language of élites
     to the language of human rights.

'Queer' has had a changing history:
It used to be the heterosexual slang of sneering dismissal.
It has more recently been revived
   as an affirmation of an identity that is both
   'peculiar' to the mainstream,
   and a revolutionary challenge to the mainstream values.
For example, it takes issue with the idols of
   the nuclear family, racial purity, religious dogmas,
   narrow nationalism, and materialism.
For some it is what Christianity is about at its best.

I may say that I *think* I was born this way,
    and *know* that it goes back a long way,
    to a time well before puberty.
But is it genetically determined?
    Am I bound to be this way,
    bound by an unalterable law of Nature?
Or might I in fact be able to choose?
Might those who claim to have been changed
    be right about that possibility?
But if so,
    why should it be thought that any one
    with any sense would choose to be heterosexual?
Cannot a choice for a same-sex relationship
    have equivalent validity, morally and spiritually?
If as a young person I know what it is
    to be deeply attracted to others of both genders,
have I not discovered that I am a human sexual
    with a variety of potential for loving?
It could happen that there would be
    much more sexual activity going on,
    both heterosexually and homosexually.
It wouldn't be a prairie fire out of control,
    but a kind of human global warming.

NB

If a gay gene were discovered,
    would fundamentalists opt for abortion?

Source: Jack Nichols, *The Gay Agenda*, Prometheus Books, 1996,with acknowledgment.

There is something that is common
  to most lesbian and gay groups,
  religious and secular,
  from campaigning groups concerned with justice
  to hidden groups concerned with support.
Each reveals the common human need for safe spaces
  in which we can be

honest with one another;

deeply accept one another;

help one another move
  from self-doubt to self-confidence,
  from self-hatred to self-love;
      (Love your neighbour *as yourself*,
      and you cannot love your neighbour
      unless you have a genuine concern
      for your own deepest well-being.)

affirm one another's worth and dignity;

encourage one another to take responsibility
  for growing up;

together tap the hidden resources
  which some would wish to call
  those of the God of unbounded love,
  inner resources of generosity and courtesy,
    of vulnerability and intimacy,
    of patience and steadiness,
  the flow of which we block by our enslavement
    to fear, guilt, and power.

Various possible responses to the question:
Are you married?

No.
  Correct, but curt.

No-one on the horizon yet.
  Irrelevant,
  and designed to put the enquirer off the scent.

No, that isn't my orientation.
  True, but sounds pompous
  and avoids plain words.

No, I'm not inclined that way.
  True, but still a bit heavy.

No, I'm gay.
  At last!

No. Actually, I'm rather like you:
I'm discreetly looking round at the men here,
and I think the best man's gorgeous, don't you?
  Invites conspiratorial laugh.

The link between sex and pleasure
 is emphasized by those who have escaped from
 the link between sex and necessary duty.

The link between sex and relationship
 is emphasized by those whose moral thinking
 wants to discover new forms of bonding
 beyond those who focused solely on
 the link between sex and procreation.

The link between sex and desire
 is emphasized by those who do not wish to limit
 the experience of sexuality to personal relationship
 but recognize it as the energy
 that impels human beings to draw close to,
 be united with, and create with
 matter in a variety of forms,
 and also so to engage with the divine.

The link between sex and immortality
 is emphasized by those who have come to terms
 with the link between sex, disease, and death,
 by those who limit their notion of immortality
 to the passing on of meaning to their children,
 and by those who believe sexual delight
 to be but a foretaste of heaven.

Four ways of experiencing life as a lesbian woman:

1   to be attracted physically and emotionally
        to other women;

2   to become soul friends sharing a profound
        inner life;

3   to bond together against hierarchies of male
        domination;

4   to give and receive practical and political
        support.

Some gay men can parallel all four,
    but many only no. 1.
Some gay men, but not as many as lesbian women -
    and indeed women as a whole - though considerably
    more than heterosexual men, know no. 2.
Some gay men (and some heterosexual men) join
    many women in 3.
Many gay men, especially in the face of AIDS,
    experience no. 4.
To most heterosexual men, all this is an alien world.

Source: Elizabeth Stuart, *Just Good Friends*, Mowbray 1995, with
acknowledgment.

An English vicar moved to Northern Ireland
   to join a community working for reconciliation.
He became publicly vocal in criticizing the Orange Order.
He was arrested at dawn.
In jail on remand boiling water was poured over him.
He was released on bail.
The charge was child molesting.
The case was later dismissed.

Those are the facts.
The possible interpretations are:
   He had indeed committed such a crime,
   harming a child by physical and emotional abuse ...
   A child, abused by somebody else,
   or an adult with memories and a grudge,
   placed (or more accurately mis-placed) an accusation ...
   He is innocent, but the simple fact of being charged
   is enough to ruin his work, and he has to move ...
   A threatened but powerful group of people
   'arranges' the arrest with police allies,
   so effectively removing the threat,
   the police then issuing an apology for their mistake ...

Few people who stand up for the rights of a minority
   or for an unpopular truth
   are immune from accusations, false or true.
And who is willing to be a completely open book?
And what is the whole truth about any person or group?

But it is an all too common human trait
   to claim to be pure and always in the right,
and so justify *any* means to use whatever power
   is at our disposal,
to exclude others from our midst.

The care of children:

1   Because you are lesbian or gay
        you know what it is like to be rejected -
        possibly when you were quite young.
    Because children needing care
        have already suffered from adults,
        they need those who recognize their need,
        have grown through their own suffering,
        and can offer empathy, affection, and encouragement.

2   No parent or guardian is likely to influence a child
        towards a sexual orientation that he or she
            is already becoming aware of.
    If gay men can model anything for children,
        it is likely to be courteous gentleness
            and appropriate anger
            rather than macho hardness and ill-temper.
    Boys in their care are very likely to grow up
        as the considerate heterosexual men
        that make the best husbands and fathers.

3   Should we not be doing what we can
        to *extend* our families to provide children
        with *several* good relationships with adults -
            relatives, neighbours, 'adopted' uncles and aunts,
            godparents, friends?
    It is a distortion from those with the mindset
        of the nuclear family
    to suppose that children in the care of lesbian
        or gay couples
    will grow up relating well only to one gender.

In a relationship between an adult and a child,
  if you deny that there is *any* element
    of sexual energy -
  and I mean that in the broadest sense,
    not in a narrowly genital sense -
you take away part of the dynamic
  of bonding and creativity
  that is needed if the child is to grow.

In a relationship between an adult and a child,
  if you deny that there is *any* element
    of spiritual energy -
  and I mean that in the broadest sense,
    not in a narrowly pious sense -
you take away part of the dynamic
  of bonding and creativity
  that is needed if the child is to grow,

and you are in danger of allowing the sexual
  to take over,
which in extreme cases can lead to
  a premature genital expression of that relationship.

The sexuality of the pre-pubescent girl or boy
  may well be in bud
  and indeed almost ripe.
(Think of thirteen year old girls being married
  at the first sign of fertility.)
But if you force a bud to open,
  you may well destroy it,
  you will at least damage it badly,
  you produce a flower that soons withers,
    and there is no fruit.

'Among baptized Christians,
   members together in the Body of Jesus Christ,
there is neither Jew nor Greek,
   male nor female,
   free nor slave.
On the contrary, there is a radical equality.

But there are some we spurn and shun,
   because we are caught up in an acknowledged
   or tacit homophobia and heterosexism.

We reject them,
   treat them as pariahs,
   and push them outside the confines
     of our church communities;
thereby we reverse that radical consequence
   of their baptism and ours.

We make them doubt that they are the children of God,
   and this must be nearly the ultimate blasphemy.
We blame them for something that it is becoming
   increasingly clear they can do little about.
Someone has said that if this particular sexual orientation were indeed a matter of personal choice,
then gay and lesbian people must be the craziest coots
   around to choose a way of life that exposes them
   to so much hostility, discrimination, loss,
     and suffering.
To say this is akin to saying that black people
   voluntarily choose a complexion and race
   that exposes them to all the hatred, suffering,
   and disadvantages to be found in a racist society.
Such people would be stark raving mad ...

[contd. on next page]

... It is only of homosexual people
  that we require universal celibacy,
  whereas for others we teach
    that celibacy is a special vocation.
We say that sexual orientation is a matter of indifference,
  but what is culpable are homosexual acts.
But then we claim that sexuality is a divine gift,
  which used properly helps us to become
    more fully human and akin to God,
  because it is this part of our humanity
    that makes us more gentle and caring,
    more self-giving and concerned for others
    than we would be without that gift.
Why should we want all homosexual people
  not to give expression to their sexuality
  in loving acts?
Why do we not use the same criteria
  to judge same-sex relationships
  that we use to judge whether heterosexual
    relationships are wholesome or not?

I am left deeply disturbed by these inconsistencies
  and know that the Lord of the Church
  would not be where his church is in this matter.
Can we act quickly to let the gospel imperatives prevail
  as we remember our baptism and theirs,
  and be thankful?

[contd. from previous page]

Source: Desmond M. Tutu, Archbishop Emeritus of Cape Town.
Adapted slightly from his Foreword to *We Were Baptized Too*,
edited by Marilyn Alexander and James Preston,
Westminster John Knox Press, Louisville, Kentucky USA, 1996
and printed here with their permission and with all rights reserved.

Originally published by the Lesbian and Gay Christian Movement to
mark its twenty-first year.

How do you know that it is no longer night
  but that a new day has dawned?

When you can distinguish a ewe from a ram?

When you can see the black and white of a border collie?

When grey turns to colours in the landscape?

Or when the unknown stranger
  who has joined you in the dark
  is recognized as your sister or brother?

11
PRAYING AND PROMISING

Dear God,
  Giver of life,
  Bearer of pain,
  Maker of love,
affirming in your incarnation
  the goodness of the flesh,
may the yearnings of our bodies
  be fulfilled in sacraments of love,
and our earthly embracings be enjoyed
  as a foretaste of the glory to come,
in the light of the Resurrection of Jesus,
  our Companion,
  our Lover,
  and our Guide.

Living God,
  Source of our being
  and Goal of our becoming,

in whose Holy Spirit of Love and Wisdom
  we live the nights and days,

by whom our wounds are healed,
  and our hurts and hurting are absorbed
  and lose their power to harm,

through whom we are drawn close to one another
  in our bodies,
    to be touched and to touch,
    to receive and to give,
    in pleasure and delight,
    in intimacy and trust,
    in tremblings of our flesh
    and in matings of our soul,

we come to rest in your stillness in gratitude,
  and to be recharged with your energy in hope,

that with deep desire rekindled
  we may follow the Way of the Maker of Love,

who embodied, once, and for all,
  your heart of Love Divine,

and with whom we swive
  in the dance of the new creation.

Occasion: The twentieth anniversary of the founding of the Lesbian and
Gay Christian Movement in 1976

Creator God,
  whose love and compassion extends to all,
  without distinction of sex or sexuality,
we offer you our lives and experience
  as gay men and lesbian women.
Help us to play our special part
  in your work of redeeming love for all people.
Give us strength to carry your love
  into a world that may reject or ignore us.
May we journey with Christ
  in faith and truth and justice.
We remember in prayer
  the communion of churches,
    that your desire for love and peace and freedom
    may be honoured by all the communities of faith ...
  lesbian women and gay men throughout the world,
    especially those oppressed by hatred, injustice,
    or imprisonment ...
  those who are lonely, confused, or suicidal ...
  those who are deprived and have no voice ...
  those who are elderly and face new fears ...
  those who live their approaching death ...
  those who care for them, and those who mourn ...
    that we may all know ourselves
    acceptable and accepted ...
  those we love, our partners, friends,
    parents, families ...
    that our love may be a reflection of yours ...
  those who seek to hurt us,
    that their hearts may be changed ...
  ourselves, that we may be ready to respond in love
    to the needs of our gay brothers and lesbian sisters
    and all your creation ...
Creator God, your love be shown in our lives:
Your will be done throughout the world.

Source: A prayer by members of the Lesbian and Gay Christian
Movement, 1996

Word made flesh! We see Christ Jesus
  Sharing our humanity,
Loving, graceful, always truthful,
  Close to others bodily,
Full of passion, full of healing,
  Touch of God to set them free.

Wonderful are these our bodies,
  Flesh and blood to touch and see,
Place of pain and contradiction,
  Yet of joy and ecstasy,
Place of passion, place of healing,
  Touched by God who sets us free.

O how glorious and resplendent,
  Fragile body you shall be,
When endued with so much beauty,
  Full of life and strong and free,
Full of vigour, full of pleasure,
  That shall last eternally.

Glory give to God the Lover,
  Grateful hearts to the Beloved,
Blessed be the Love between them,
  Overflowing to our good:
Adoration and thanksgiving
  To the God whose Name is Love.

Source: Verses 1,2, & 4 are by the author; the third verse is late fifteenth
century, translated from the Latin by J. M. Neale, and now part of the hymn
'Light's abode, celestial Salem', *New English Hymnal* 401, to the tune 'Regent
Square'

I vow to you, my friends of earth,
  all worldly things above,
Entire and whole - yet broken -
  the service of my love:
The love that dares to question,
  the love that speaks its name,
That flowers still in barren ground,
  yet hides no more for shame:
The love that struggles through the pain,
  and whispers in the night,
Yet shares its secret with the world,
  to bring the truth to light.

This is that 'other country'
  we heard of long ago,
When called to be the spies of God
  where milk and honey flow,
A world where hurts find healing,
  where all the oppressed run free,
Where friends who have been sore betrayed
  each other truly see:
It is our earth, transfigured, new,
  where wars and hatred cease,
Where spy and friend walk hand in hand
  in Christ our Lover's Peace.

With a debt, via inspiration and irritation, to Cecil Spring-Rice who wrote
the hymn, *I vow to thee, my country*.

A Covenant of God with Humanity

I Who Am and Who Shall Be,

Love-Making Spirit within you,

Pain-Bearing Presence beside you,

Life-Giving Future before you,

I call you into being

and bind myself to you.

By my own name and nature,

in every eternal moment,

I affirm and renew my covenant,

I fulfil my deepest promise,

to love you to glory for ever,

to honour you as my home,

and to be loyal to you

and full of faith in you,

our life-day long.

Amen. So be it.

My Covenant with God

Beloved and faithful Creator,

Love-Making Spirit within me,

Pain-Bearing Presence beside me,

Life-Giving Future before me,

of my own free will

I choose to share my life with you.

This day and all my days

I affirm and renew my covenant,

I fulfil my deepest promise,

to love you in friendship for ever,

to honour you as my home,

and to be loyal to you

and full of faith in you,

our life-day long.

Amen. So be it.

A Covenant of Friendship

In the wonderful Mystery of God,

Love-Making Spirit between us,

Pain-Bearing Presence beside us,

Life-Giving Future before us,

you have been given to me,

to be cherished in friendship.

Of my own free will

I choose to share my life with you.

With and in that greater Love

I promise to do all that I can

for your well-being for as long as I shall live,

to honour you as God's home,

and to be loyal to you

and full of faith in you,

our life-day long.

Amen. So be it.

How might that promise read in a rite of passage,
   when the friendship has become a relationship
      to be acknowledged before witnesses,
      either for their contribution by law,
      or for their support to the two people concerned?
The relationship is also in the public sphere
   because property is usually being shared,
   because bank accounts may be held jointly,
   because wills have been drawn up,
and also, and more significantly for everybody concerned,
   the relationship of the couple
      with their families and friends
      changes from that moment on.
As in any rite of passage,
   especially if it is in principle or in reality
      a once-in-a-lifetime event,
   people become or stop being
      a couple, a grandparent, a widower, etc.
When a friend of yours takes a partner,
   your relationship to that friend changes.
You may or may not get to know the partner,
   but the fact of that partnership
      has to be built into the way in which
      that friendship shifts, loosens, or flourishes.
And many friendships go into suspension,
   sometimes for years,
   sometimes until the couple's children
      have grown up and left home.
On the whole,
   friendships are conducted in the private sphere,
   even if there are more or less formal arrangements
      about property, finance, and inheritance.
None of these are an integral part of friendship,
   but one or more of them
   is usually an integral part of partnership,
   whether that be marriage or some other kind.

Some lesbian and gay people want
   the right to be 'married',
to be able to have their relationship
   recognized as such by the law
   and blessed as such by the Church.
Some, as with some heterosexual people,
   want 'registered partnerships'
   or some kind of recognition as 'cohabitees'.
Many are very suspicious of the model. Why?

Women still experience marriage as unequal:
   men usually have the power and money ...
The average span of a marriage in the UK is nine years ...
Two-thirds of married people have
   other sexual relationships as well ...
Younger people cohabit
   and many older people go largely
   separate ways after child-rearing ...
People do not want to feel inferior
   by being classified as those who fall short
   of an ideal which seems to be an idol ...
Until 1000 only the marriages of clergy
   and the wealthy were blessed ...
Two hundred years ago, only half the population
   in the UK were formally married ...
When there was a contract,
   it was between two male owners of the woman,
   her father and her husband,
and it was needed to ensure that property
   was smoothly transferred and the eldest son inherited ...
The privacy of marriage puts it largely beyond justice:
   the notion of marital rape is very recent ...
When you ask the happily married
   what makes their relationship work
   they usually reply that they are the best of friends ...

Source: Elizabeth Stuart, *Just Good Friends*, Mowbray 1995, with acknowledgment.

Friendships

are between *kin*dred spirits -
the bodily bond being often stronger
  than among one's kith and *kin* -
across the separations of
  class, race, gender, creed;

are mutual in encouragement and critique,
  in support and challenge;

are informed by diffuse sexual energy,
  which may or may not find focus
  in one particular other person
  who becomes central and primary;

are rumoured to be God's apology for relations ...

Pat, aged 35, and Chris, aged 22,
  wish to be married in church.
Both are baptised Christians,
  though neither is a regular communicant.
Neither has been married before.
They have put down a deposit on a flat in your parish
  and hope they will have access to it a month or so
  before their marriage.
Pat has lived locally in rented accommodation
  for the past six years,
  and works for the local council
  in the accounts department.
Chris has been living at the family home
  in a city a hundred miles away
  while studying commercial design.
The course has just ended,
  and Chris has secured a job with an advertising agency
  in a town some ten miles from your parish.

How do your emotional, ethical, and pastoral responses
  vary if:

Pat is a man and Chris is a woman?

Chris is a man and Pat is a woman?

Pat and Chris are both women?

Pat and Chris are both men?

A day of blessing,
    a day to focus all your nights and days,
    as intense as sunlight focused through a glass,
    as ordinary as sunlight's daily warmth.

A day of blessing,
    that declares that your love for each other is good,
    that publishes it, through us your witnesses,
        to the world.

A day of blessing,
    that brings into the light of day
    what has so banefully and for so long
    been buried and obscure.

A day of blessing
    that banishes fear
    and celebrates with open joy.

A day of each a blessing to the other,
    of declaring each to other
    that the love you share is very good
    and binds you close.

A day of blessing
    of all the hidden creativity between you
    and within each of you, as yet unknown,
    to flower in the maturing of love's surprise.

A day of blessing,
    in and through all these things,
    by the Divine Creator-Lover,
    a blessing full of wonder and of laughter.

A voice from heaven was heard,
    These are my beloved in whom I take great delight.

An Introduction to a Ceremony of Blessing

In the presence of God
    we have come together to give public witness
      and personal support to N and N,
    as they celebrate the love they have for each other,
    as they affirm and deepen
      their commitment to each other,
    and as they seek and receive God's blessing and ours.
In this ceremony
    we remind ourselves of what it means to be human,
    which is to grow in love for God and for one another,
    to be marked by the true love
      which draws away from self as centre,
    and towards others in mutual giving and receiving,
      in respect and compassion,
    and which teaches us to avoid all violation of the other,
      whether by force or manipulation,
      by treating the other as less than human,
      or by exploiting the other's goodwill.
From the earliest times men and women
    have made solemn vows.
The stories of David and Jonathan, of Ruth and Naomi,
    remind us of such promises made before God
    and calling on God to witness and bless the love
    they swore to each other for ever.
We have come to witness
    another such exchange of promises,
    because we believe that God, who is Love and Truth,
      and sees deep into the human heart,
      longs to bless N and N,
      recognizes the love that they have for each other,
      accepts the offering they are making,
      longs to see them flourish and grow in their love,
      and to shower them with all that is good.

Questions of intent:

N and N, you are about to make a solemn promise.

Do you believe that God has called you to live together
   in ever deepening love for each other?
      We do.

Do you promise to be loyal to each other,
   never allowing any other relationship
   to come before the one you are now to affirm?
      We do.

Will you give yourselves to each other wholeheartedly
   and without reserve?
      We will.

Will you, under God, recognize each other's freedom
   and allow each other time and space
   to grow into that unique being each of us is called to be?
      We will.

Will you do all in your power to make your life together
   a witness to the love of God in the world?
      We will.

N, will you give yourself to N,
   sharing your love and your life,
   your strengths and your weaknesses,
   your well-being and your brokenness,
   your health and your sickness,
   your riches and your poverty,
   your success and your failure,
   through all the days that are given to you?
      I will.

Questions of intent
    in the early days of a relationship, for a period
      of growing together,
      of testing,
      of sounding the depths.

N and N,
    God loves you.
    How do you respond?
        We wish to grow in love,
        sharing more and more of our lives
        with each other,
        and we seek God's blessing.

Will you, within your life together,
    give each other room to breathe and grow,
    each in your own way?
        We will.

Your relationship has not yet been tested
    by time or trouble.
Will you try to make it a strong and durable one?
        We will.

If you decide not to stay together,
    will you try to part in goodwill,
    with forgiveness, and without bitterness?
        We will.

God is the source of love.
    Will you accept that gift,
    sharing it with each other
    and with those around you?
        We will.

A Covenant of Special Friendship

In the wonderful Mystery of God,
Love-Making Spirit between us,
Pain-Bearing Presence beside us,
Life-Giving Future before us,

you have been given to me,
to be cherished in a special friendship,
to share with you all that I have and all that I am,
with a loyalty to you that comes before all others.

Of my own free will
I choose to share my life with you,
(and to care for such children
as may be entrusted to us).

With and in that greater Love,
and in the presence of these our witnesses,

I affirm, renew, and deepen my promise

to do all that I can for your well-being
for as long as I shall live,

to honour you as God's home,

and to be loyal to you
and full of faith in you,
our life-day long.

Amen. So be it.

Exchange of rings or other gifts

Prayer:

God of generosity and bounty,
   bless these rings
   which we also bless in your name.
May N and N who will wear them
   recognize these symbols
   of the love that never ends.
May they find gladness in each other,
   in mutual giving and receiving,
   in the ringed dance of love.
May they be glad in the gift of their bodies,
   in touch and passion,
   in affection and goodwill.
May they bring to each other tact and generosity,
   compassion and forgiveness,
May they share their joys and their sufferings,
   their fears and their trust,
each giving the other room to grow
   in freedom and in truth.

Exchange:

This ring is a symbol
   of never-ending love,
   of all that I am
   and all that I have.
Receive and treasure it
   as a token and pledge
   of the love I have for you.
Wear it always,
   and find in it a protection
   whenever we have to be apart.

Prayer of Offering

Living God,
  Creator and Lover of the world,
we offer our lives to you this day,
  and our life together in you,
all our words and deeds,
  our hopes and fears,
  and our amazing love.
Accept us as we are,
  with all our stumbling
  and with all our courage.
Guide us into what you have us be.
And in the power of your Spirit
  enable us to be a sign of your presence in the world,
after the pattern
  and in the name
  of Jesus your true and well Beloved.

Prayer of Blessing

Spirit of the living God,
   strengthen N and N,
   that they may persevere in love,
   grow in mutual understanding,
   and give to each other in ever-deepening trust.
Shower them with your gifts
   of wisdom, patience, and courage,
   that their love may be a source of happiness
   and their home a place of welcome
   for all who are their guests.

God the Giver of Life,
God the Bearer of Pain,
God the Maker of Love,
   bless, preserve, and keep you.
The light of God shine upon you,
   guide you in truth and peace,
   and make you strong in love and faith,
that you may grow together in this life,
   and your love be taken up even beyond death itself,
   and be transfigured to glory.

Bidding to the Witnesses

Will you,
   N and N's chosen witnesses this day,
   do everything in your power
   to support and encourage them
   in the years ahead,
   quietly being there for them
   in times of stress and sorrow,
   with laughter being there for them
   in times of celebration and joy?

      We will.

God has called us in the Spirit of friendship
   to live in peace.
Let us share with N and N
   and with one another
   a greeting of peace.

The Shalom of the living God embrace you:

      The peace of the living God touch your heart.

What do you mean when you say,
  'I love you'?

  'I fancy you: you turn me on.'

  'I could listen to you all night.'

  'My hero ...'

  'I'm lonely and I need to defy the dark.'

  'I'm starved of touch.'

To say,
  I ... love ... you
is to acknowledge that you are
  unique,
  different from me,
  multi-layered,
  open to vast possibilities of becoming,
  for ever a mystery.
It is to give you my whole attention
  so that I love you,
and not a projection of what I like or want or need.

You are a painting waiting to be discovered,
a poem waiting to be written,
a piece of music waiting to be played,
a song waiting to be sung.

Love's Persistence

Love is patient and kind
and knows no envy.

Love never clings,
is never boastful, conceited, or rude.

Love is never selfish,
never insists on its own way.

Love is not quick to take offence.

Love keeps no score of wrongs,
nor gloats over the sins of others.

Love rejoices in the truth.

Love is tough:
there is nothing it cannot face.

Love never loses trust
in human beings or in God.

Love never loses hope,
never loses heart.

Love still stands
when all else has fallen.

Three things last for ever:
faith, hope, and love -

and it is love that crowns them all.

Source: 1 Corinthians 13

The Way of Love

Love your enemies.

Do good to those who hate you.

Bless those who curse you.

Pray for those who abuse you.

Do good and lend,
  expecting nothing in return.

For God is kind
  even to the ungrateful and selfish.

Be merciful
  as your father is merciful.

Judge not,
  and you will not be judged.

Condemn not,
  and you will not be condemned.

Forgive,
  and you will be forgiven.

Give,
  and gifts will be given to you.

The measure you give
  will be the measure you receive.

Source: The Gospel according to Luke chapter 6

Dwelling in Love

If you dwell in the Divine Love,
if you join the Dance of the Three-in-One,
the Lover,
the Beloved,
the Mutual Friend,
if you are caught up in the Love
that is generous and overflowing,

you will find yourself loving and being loved
with the whole of your being,
loving your neighbour as yourself,
and loving even your enemy;

and, as surely as night follows day,
you will never use force -
though you will refuse to let others
escape from the demands of love and truth;
you will never use others
merely to provide what you want -
though you will respect and acknowledge
your own needs;
you will never take advantage
of others' ignorance or immaturity -
though you will try to increase their knowledge
and wisdom.

The Adverbs of Love

Love others, and receive their love -

   passionately, on wings of flame;

   fiercely, eager for truth;

   honestly, without illusion;

   courageously, bearing the hurts;

   gently, with no hint of cruelty;

   sensitively, giving room to breathe;

   respectfully, without possessing;

   responsibly, aware of consequences;

   trustfully, without fear of rejection;

   welcomingly, without demanding change;

   forgivingly, open to being reconciled;

   generously, without thought of return;

   wholeheartedly, full of faith and loyalty.

Love your Enemies

Neither condemn nor destroy your enemies.

Keep in contact with them -
  even if you cannot keep 'in touch'.

Strive powerfully with them,
  struggling shoulder to shoulder,
  until you see each other face to face.

Be angry with compassion, not with hatred.

Do not yield to bitterness or fury.

Be strongly and persuasively gentle -
  with others and with yourself.

Where there is icy hatred in your heart,
  let it be melted by the warmth of goodwill.

Do not meet oppression with violation -
  for we have all been too much hurt.

Your enemies are human beings like yourself:
  do not picture them as less than human,
  and refuse all propaganda that distorts.

And keep a sense of proportion -
  and a sense of humour.

With expanding heart,
  love your enemies.

When issues of sexuality surface,
   and especially when they do so for the first time,
there is usually an excess of emotion,
   raised voices,
   a lot of noise.
This raising of the temperature is vital,
   and should not be cooled prematurely.
But when the energy inevitably has spent itself,
   then is the time to

Listen ...

   to the fragile feelings,
      not to the clashing fury ...

   to the quiet sounds,
      not to the loud clamour ...

   to the steady heartbeat,
      not to the noisy confusion ...

   to the hidden voices,
      not to the obvious chatter ...

   to the deep harmonies,
      not to the surface discord ...

A slow turning
A gentle roasting
A transformation into succulence ...

Puncture my bloated pride:
    sow the hidden seed of humility.

Root out my cruel and bitter anger:
    sow the hidden seed of courtesy.

Disentangle me from the web of envy:
    sow the hidden seed of justice.

Make clear the hypocrisies of my lust:
    sow the hidden seed of truth.

Take from my heart my grasping after money:
    sow the hidden seed of generosity.

Still my gluttonous pursuit of pleasure:
    sow the hidden seed of charity.

Penetrate the fog of my sloth:
    sow the hidden seed of laughter.

'We are only just now beginning
   to look upon the relation of one individual person
      to a second individual
      objectively and without prejudice,
and our attempts to live such associations
   have no model before them ...

(but) some day there will be girls and women
   whose name will no longer signify
      merely an opposite of the masculine,
   but something in itself,
   something that makes one think,
      not of any complement or limit,
      but only of life and existence:
      the feminine human being.

This advance ... will change the love-experience,
   which is now full of error,
   will alter it from the ground up,
   reshape it into a relation that is meant to be
      of one human being to another,
   no longer of man to woman.

And this more human love
   (which will fulfil itself,
      infinitely considerate and gentle,
      and kind and clear in binding and releasing)
   will resemble that which we are preparing
      with struggle and toil,
   the love that consists in this,
   that two solitudes
      protect and border and salute each other,
      (guard and touch and greet each other).'

Source: R. M. Rilke, *Letters to a Young Poet*, Norton, New York, 1934, 1954,
pp. 58-9, the last line being an alternative translation. With acknowledgment.

Fall in love with God ...

Why do you hesitate?
  Reserve?
  Thinking that a jealous God
    will make you give up human loving?
  Living with a picture of God
    as Controller and Policeman?

After all, to fall in love is to lose control.

But may be God is not a puppeteer,
  wanting to monitor your every movement.

Maybe God is sure and steady love -
  desiring intimacy with you and for you,
  desiring justice among us all:
God-is-for-us,
God-is-with-us,
God-is-for-our-well-being.

God desires you to flourish,
God enjoys dancing with you,
God is revealed to you in the midst of your loving.

God is absolutely intimate,
  within each of us, totally understanding.
God is absolutely beyond,
  other than any of us, totally challenging.

God is the Mysterious Other Within.

Open your heart and mind, your imagination and flesh
  to this Impossible Beauty.

Fall in love with God.

What kind of love do we seek?

The love that is without limits:

> The one who loves accepts
> that the other may well hurt
> and even try to destroy.
> But nothing that the other can do
> will ever be able to defeat love.

The love that does not control:

> The one who loves accepts
> that love is precarious
> and that tragedy may occur,
> yet always works to redeem
> rather than to take revenge,
> and there is no tragedy
> that is beyond that transforming power.

The love that is not detached:

> The one who loves accepts that
> deep involvement with another
> means constant exposure
> and constant vulnerability.

No limits.
No control.
No withdrawal.

Source: W. H. Vanstone, *Love's Endeavour, Love's Expense*, Darton, Longman, and Todd, 1977, with acknowledgment.

Shakespeare knew well the consolation of friendship:

When in disgrace with fortune and men's eyes
I all alone beweep my outcast state,
And trouble deaf heaven with my bootless cries,
And look upon myself, and curse my fate,
Wishing me like to one more rich in hope,
Featur'd like him, like him with friends possess'd,
Desiring this man's art, and that man's scope,
With what I most enjoy contented least;
Yet in these thoughts myself almost despising,
Haply I think on thee - and then my state,
Like to the lark at break of day arising
From sullen earth, sings hymns at heaven's gate;
   For thy sweet love remember'd such wealth brings
   That then I scorn to change my state with Kings.

Source: William Shakespeare, *Sonnet XXIX*

Shakespeare knew well the perils of
  inordinate sexual desire:

Th'expense of Spirit in a waste of shame
Is lust in action; and till action, lust
Is perjured, murderous, bloody, full of blame,
Savage, extreme, rude, cruel, not to trust;
Enjoy'd no sooner but despised straight;
Past reason hunted; and, no sooner had,
Past reason hated, as a swallow'd bait
On purpose laid to make the taker mad;
Mad in pursuit, and in possession so;
Had, having, and in quest to have, extreme;
A bliss in proof, and proved, a very woe;
Before a joy proposed; behind, a dream.
  All this the world well knows; yet none knows well
  To shun the heaven that leads men to this hell.

Source: William Shakespeare, *Sonnet CXXIX*

Shakespeare knew well the challenges to love's endurance:

Let me not to the marriage of true minds
Admit impediments. Love is not love
Which alters when it alteration finds,
Or bends with the remover to remove:
O no! it is an ever-fixed mark
That looks on tempests and is never shaken;
It is the star to every wandering bark,
Whose worth's unknown, although his height is taken.
Love's not Time's fool, though rosy lips and cheeks
Within his bending sickle's compass come:
Love alters not with his brief hours and weeks,
But bears it out even to the edge of doom.
  If this be error and upon me proved,
  I never writ, nor no man ever loved.

Source: William Shakespeare, *Sonnet CXVI*

He brought light out of darkness,
   not out of a lesser light;
he can bring thy summer out of winter,
   though thou have no spring;
though in the ways of fortune,
   or understanding, or conscience
thou have been benighted till now,
   wintred and frozen,
   clouded and eclypsed,
   damped and benummed,
   smothered and stupified till now,
now God comes to thee,
   not as in the dawning of the day,
   but as the sun at noon to illustrate all shadowes,
   as the sheaves in harvest,
   to fill all penuries,
   all occasions invite his mercies,
   and all times are his seasons.

Source: John Donne, Sermon on Isaiah 7.14, St Paul's Cathedral, London, Christmas Day 1624

You cannot know true love
  if you are possessed by the spirit of domination.
I am not loving you
  if I am dominating you,
  exercising my power over you,
  forcing myself upon you.
I must resist the temptation to push and impose.
To do so I have to learn to be silent,
  learn to give space.

You cannot know true love
  if you are dominated by the spirit of possession.
I am not loving you
  if I am possessing you,
  becoming possessive of you,
  clinging to you.
I must resist the temptation to pull and crush.
To do so I have to learn to give space,
  learn to be silent.

I seek a way of loving you
  without dominating or possessing you,
  and without fusing with you.
For there to be the union and creativity
  that is the fulfilment of sexual longing,
there must be room to breathe between us.

So I need to learn what it means
  to be silent,
  to allow an empty space,
  to enter into solitude.

Then I may be able to give shape to our loving,
  and to be open to the unknown that is to come.
Our love may then become sacramental,
  fully embodied and fully spirited,
  conveying meaning to each other.

To love solitude is not to hate flesh, sex, or people.

For May Sarton, American lesbian poet and novelist,
  it was always a struggle to find time for her real work,
  for the receptive state of mind that makes it possible,
  for the deep inner space for creativity.

She wrote of solitude,
  like a long love,
  deepening with time.

Solitude is about detachment,
  not about being a recluse.
It was a matter of not allowing herself
  to be pulled out of her own orbit
  by violent attraction,
of being able to enjoy
  without needing to possess.

An intimate relationship need not get in the way,
The cake to be divided up
  will not be commitment,
  but time,
    some of it together,
    much of it alone.

Rainer Maria Rilke echoes May Sarton.

He recognized that even in the closest intimacy,
  infinite spaces exist between the two human beings.
Once they can accept that fact,
  a wonderful living side by side can grow.
But they have to learn to love the distances between them
  which alone make it possible
  for each to see the other whole
  and against a wide sky.

Creative work needs a large generous solitude,
  long contented draughts of solitude
  drunk deep over hours at a time.

But for him such work springs from the sexual,
  is of one nature with it:
it is like a gentler, but ecstatic, repetition of delight.
'In one creative thought
  a thousand forgotten nights of love revive
  and fill it with sublimity and exaltation ...'

Source: R. M. Rilke, *Letters to a Young Poet*, Norton, New York, 1934, 1954, with acknowledgment.

Sexual solitude is a loving and creative place to be
   only if we know from the inside
   that sexual desire is good,
   that sexual union is to be welcomed,
   that inner creativity depends on being in touch
     with sexual energy.
Otherwise the solitude will degenerate
   into isolation and bitterness.
Every creative work of art
   calls upon the memories of sexual union,
   of the creative energy thus released,
even if those sexual acts
   are those of our ancestors
   or of our contemporaries
   who nourish us in our solitude
   with the creativity that is their gift to us.
There may even be moments in solitude
   of heightened awareness,
   of passionate engagement with the material
     of one's art,
   of gestating and wrestling and birthing,
that give to the whole-flesh-body
   an intense yet diffused excitement and glow,
   a pleasure of which orgasm is
   but a momentary shiver of a reflection.

12
Remembering and Reaching

The churches have never been totally happy
   about bodies, flesh, matter,
but have just about held on to the conviction
   that they are not actually evil.
However, from time to time,
   various groups have sprung up
   claiming that all matter is indeed evil.
Logically of course this means that
   they have nothing to do with sex
   and so rapidly become extinct.
One such movement was in southern France
   in the twelfth and thirteenth centuries.
It was called the Albigensian heresy.
Because procreation keeps matter alive,
   all sex is to be frowned on,
but sex that is clearly not procreative
   is not as bad as that which is.
So you can see how 'buggery' came to
   be associated with 'heresy',
and indeed one possible origin of the word
   'buggery' is from the French 'bougre',
   which means 'heretic'.

Models from the past that may have value:

Modern society limits the idea of 'covenant' to marriage.
Ancient society extended the idea of 'covenant' to
     include not only marriage but also
     an affectionate bond between two men or two women,
     political alliance, and a relationship with God.
A covenant is characterized by
     keeping the bonds of affection in good repair,
     being obliged to further the welfare of each other,
     keeping faith with the terms of the agreement,
          which, while it may be legal and public,
          puts the personal above the formal,
     bringing together friendship and kinship.

The modern *household* is private and small.
The ancient household was large with porous boundaries,
     its web of commitments not based on marriage
          or biological relationships.
The social bonding was strong
     and mutual financial support was characteristic.
Monastic households carried this reality
     into the medieval world.
A few modern churches put into practice
     the kind of friendships that create new kinship bonds.

The *mentoring* relationship between
     teacher and pupil, skilled worker and apprentice,
     can even now be a warm and deep bonding.
A professional musician cannot teach a pupil
     unless a steady and enduring rapport is established.

The classic understanding of romantic love
     was of an appreciation of *beauty* -
     of the human form, of creation, of God -
     which called forth a response,
     which may or may not involve a sexual relationship.

If procreation is the only legitimate purpose
of sexual intercourse,
and if the new human being is thought to exist
in miniature entirely in the male seed,
it is not surprising that
there is little mention of women in teachings or laws,
there is no mention of sex as a binding power of love,
contraception is always wrong,
masturbation can even be thought more wicked than rape.

Add to this the view
that the loss of control and the failure of the will
is inherent in the ecstasy and frenzy of the sexual act,
and that the flesh,
whether as the whole of life organized against God
or specificially as sexual desire as lust and out of control
is thought to be the most obvious way
that evil finds an entrance into human life.
Also add to this the need for the Church
to establish its distinctiveness
(which, unlike Judaism, it did not do via laws about food).

It is then easy to understand that our ancestors
would have been horrified
at much contemporary *conservative* thinking that
sex is good and helps to bind a relationship,
sexual desire can be the servant of love,
self-abandonment to the other is to be encouraged,
contraception can be acceptable,
there is little or no fuss about masturbation
and in practice not much about oral sex.

However, all these changes can be made
within a framework of heterosexual monogamy:
lesbian and gay relationships
(as deliberately childless marriages)
sever the at least potential link with procreation.

The Christian tradition about sex is mixed.
Erotic love is celebrated in the Song of Songs,
   though it has often been interpreted as an allegory,
   that is, a way of drawing parallels that don't meet,
   in this case between the human and the divine.
But it has also been interpreted as a parable,
   that is, a sample of a love that includes
     but goes beyond the human.

Genesis *can* be understood as signifying that
   the union and intimacy of two becoming one flesh
   is more important than procreation.

Jesus himself challenged purity rules:
   uncleanness does not imply immorality
   and should not be used to exclude.

But we have heard loudest and longest the associations of
   dualism,
   disgust,
   decay,
   danger,
   dirt,
   disease,
   death,
   don't.

And the male élites lifted themselves -
   at least they did in theory -
   above nature, sex, earth, woman,
   exalting celibacy as a mark of the first-class Christian.
And male clergy, frustrated sexually,
   turned to power games,
   using their position and wealth over against others,
   that is, women, heretics, Jews, and Muslims,
and they invented the reluctant necessity approach to sex.

Our ancestors of the first centuries of the common era
   are strangers to us, their backs towards us.

For them nature was hostile,
   and sex was bound up with danger, disease, and death,
   with that which is out of human control.
Therefore human beings had surely to rise above it.

It is not that they were completely anti-sex.
   They weren't stupid:
   sexual coupling is vital to survival;
   marriage is held in respect and family life honoured.
But once you can no longer have children, be abstinent.

The male body was held in honour.
   Men were not to be effeminate in deportment
   because they would then be 'liquid' - like women.
Clement of Alexandria contrasted 'uncontrolled guffaws'
   with 'the slow melodious chuckle of the saints'.
Behaviour, manner of life, and body were
   to be sanctified as much as spirit.
So there were rules for how to sit,
   how to burp (gently),
   and whether to scratch the ears (refrain).
The body was the soul's 'consort and ally'.

So our ancestors did not hate or denounce the body.
To us they may sound reluctant and grudging about sex,
   but they were not completely inhumane.

Source: Peter Brown, *The Body and Society*, Faber, 1989, with
acknowledgment.

Perhaps we could say that the Church
  of those early centuries slowly sidelined sex.
They did emphasize the break with the past
  when a person was baptized,
  and used the language of purity.
  Baptism was better at giving a shine
  than any washing powder or fuller's earth.
  Neither clothes nor body should be besmirched.
  This came down to us as a question to boys:
  Do you sleep with your hands under the bedclothes?
  Remember that Christian hands don't stray.
Origen taught that to be bodily but not sexual
  was more completely to reflect the purity of the soul
  and therefore to be closer to God.
That is illustrated by the gradual restriction of leadership
  first to the married but abstinent
  and then to the unmarried and abstinent.
  Ninety-eight percent of the quotations in the new
  Catholic Catechism are by celibate men.
For Ambrose of Milan celibate clergy and virgins
  are signs to the world of their spiritual authority.
  Like Christ they are 'unmixed'.
  The body may not be evil, but it is perilous.
The supposed virginal conception of Jesus
  avoids the impurities of the process.
Augustine of Hippo believed
  that the human will is distorted,
  which in turn leads to a distortion of the sexual impulse.
The impulse is not evil,
  but cannot be experienced without sinning.
  So intercourse is linked with the transmission
    of original sin.
  'Fettered by the flesh's morbid impulses
  and lethal sweetness, I dragged my chain.'

Sources: Peter Brown, *The Body and Society*, Faber, 1989, with acknowledgment;
Augustine of Hippo, *Confessions* VI. xii. 21

In early medieval Europe,
  up to the thirteenth century,
male sexual attraction to other men was not thought
  odd,
  immoral,
  grounds for stigmatizing.

Aelred of Rievaulx, a Cistercian monk,
  wrote of it in the twelfth century
    without embarrassment,
    without censure,
    without arguing against an opposition.

So there is no consistent and persistent opposition
  throughout Christian history.

As a word, sodomy had not yet been coined:
  Sodom, according to Ezekiel 16.49-50,
  was destroyed for its pride, luxury, and injustice.

Perspectives and policies therefore have shifted:
  it is only the study of history that can convince us of this.

Source: John Boswell, *Christianity, Social Tolerance, and Homosexuality*, Chicago University Press, 1980, with acknowledgment.

There are sixty extant manuscripts
  of celebrations of same-sex partnerships
  between the eighth and the seventeenth centuries.
They demonstrate a similar sequence
  and similar customs
  to marriage ceremonies.
Prayers refer to Saints Sergius and Bacchus,
  soldiers in the imperial household
  at the end of the third and beginning of the fourth
    centuries.
The ceremony is entitled 'the making of brothers'.
  'Brother' could mean more than simply kin:
  it could and did have sexual overtones.
It is specifically stated to be 'against nature',
  but this is not thought to be a bar to the relationship.
As with early Christian marriage rites,
  what was being done was to bless a relationship
  already accepted by the wider community,
  not creating that relationship in the first place.
We may argue as to the exact kinds of touch implied,
  but that same-sex relationships were
    special,
    accepted,
    and blessed,
  is quite clear.

Source: John Boswell, *Same-Sex Unions in Pre-Modern Europe*, Villard Books, New York, 1994, with acknowledgment.

Of various people from history:
    Were they or weren't they?
    Did they or didn't they?
I'm not bothered about labels
    that may or may not be a reading back into the past
    from our present categories.
I'm not bothered if the answer to the second question is,
    Probably, No they didn't.
I'm quite content to recognize some special ancestors who
    loved each other passionately,
    loved each other as embodied beings,
    sometimes shared a home,
    who were more special to each other than to anyone else.
What antics they did or did not get up to
    matters much less.
There are many kinds of 'consummation',
    and none that satisfy us for ever.
All of which is not to take away from our questions:
    If they did, why should that in itself be any concern?
    Whether they did or did not,
      how accepting was the society in which they lived?
    And how accepting is ours?

'The fact that gay people will always be in a minority
in the human community
places them permanently in a precarious position.
They are always likely to be on the edge,
prone to persecution and misunderstanding.
This may be why so many gay people,
in spite of the attacks of Christians,
are so drawn to Jesus
and his invitation to the heavy laden
to come to him and find rest for their souls.
It is humbling that so many of them choose
to remain in the Church,
in spite of its ambivalent attitude to them.
It would be fitting if the Church
acknowledged its debt to them,
sought forgiveness from them,
stopped arguing about them,
started listening to them,
and left time to heal the wounds
it has inflicted upon them.
Homosexuals are classic people of the edge,
perpetual minorities,
permanently marginalized by the majority
in the Church and in society.
This is why many of them are drawn to Jesus,
the man on the edge;
and there can be little doubt
that he would be drawn to them.'

Source: Richard Holloway, Bishop of Edinburgh, *Dancing on the Edge*,
Darton, Longman & Todd, 1997, p. 155, with acknowledgment and thanks.

How does a society become a *persecuting* society?

In eleventh and twelfth century Europe
warrior barons in feudal fiefdoms struggled for power
   against a new clerical class in budding nation states.
The new élite wished to marginalize the intelligent or
   the wealthy who threatened their position.
They tapped into the common human fears of
   disorder and *pollution*.

So heretics, lepers, sodomites, and, later, witches,
   were identified,
even if most of them were never any real threat.
There was also the attempt to destroy
   the identity of the Jews,
whose resources and abilities were a more obvious threat.

Persecution may be sporadic, occasional,
   and aimed at individuals.
Or it may become deliberately systemic,
   violence that is organized, sanctioned,
   aimed at every member of particular groups,
   and working through the institutions
     of government and law.
Membership of a racial or religious group,
   or classification by disease or way of life,
   is deemed sufficient to justify such attacks.

In our own day,
   people who are black, disabled, Jewish,
   mentally handicapped, elderly and dependent,
   sexually variant, or live with AIDS,
are on the receiving end of
   the fear of strangers, of variety, of complexity,
   the processes of stigmatizing and scapegoating,
   the confusions about where authority lies.

Source: R. I. Moore, *The Formation of a Persecuting Society*, Blackwell, 1987, with acknowledgment.

Nobody has better expressed the terrible consequences
    of oppression,
not least the forgotten silence of the oppressed,
than H. T. Buckle, writing in 1857:

'That religious persecution
    is a greater evil than any other is apparent
    not so much from the enormous
      and almost incredible number of its known victims,
    as from the fact that the unknown
      must be far more numerous,
    and that history gives no account
      of those who have been spared in the body,
      in order that they might suffer in the mind.
We hear much of martyrs and confessors -
    of those who were slain by the sword
    or consumed by the fire;
but we know little of that still larger number who,
    by the mere threat of persecution,
    have been driven into an outward abandonment
      of their true opinions;
and who, thus forced into an apostasy the heart abhors,
    have passed the remainder of their lives
    in the practice of a constant and humiliating hypocrisy.
It is this which is the real curse of persecution.
For in this way,
    men being constrained to mask their thoughts,
    there arises a habit of securing safety by falsehood,
    and of purchasing immunity by deceit.'

Source: H. T. Buckle, *History of Civilization in England*, 1857, with
acknowledgment.

Of all tyrannies,
   a tyranny exercised for the good of its victims
   may be the most oppressive.
To be 'cured' against one's will
   and cured of states we may not regard as disease,
is to be put on the level of those
   who have not yet reached the age of reason.

Source: C. S. Lewis, I think in something he wrote in about 1960, with acknowledgment.

Caution:

If there is a combination of
  a threat to national identity or security,
  internal economic and social dislocation,
  and natural disasters or epidemics,

any distinctive minority is in danger:

> Christians in the Roman Empire;
>
> Jews in medieval and modern Europe;
>
> Gypsies throughout Europe;
>
> Communists in America in the fifties;
>
> buggers and heretics in medieval Europe;
>
> black people in modern Britain;
>
> homosexual men and gypsies in
>   eighteenth century Holland.

Yes, there is always the need for high boundaries
  to protect legitimate privacies,
  to give time for seedlings to grow,
  to allow for the slow maturing of ideas and plans,
  to give space and freedom for young children to explore,
  to provide safety and hospitality for those in danger.

At our mature best, those boundaries can be lower,
  those being protected not needing to fear invasion,
  and all of us being encouraged to cross boundaries,
  to our mutual delight and education,
  each group secure in its identity,
  and each known to all with no discrimination.

Making a choice that is
　　different from the 'norm'
　　feeds the impetus to make all of life
　　different from the 'norm' -
where that 'norm' is
　　convention and conformity,
　　domination as one of the powers that be,
　　submission as one of the powerless.
The lesbian and gay exploration is
　　open to diversity,
　　characterized, at its best, by mutuality -

and that mutuality is easier to achieve
　　than in heterosexual relationships
　　with all their inherited assumptions
　　of male superiority and ownership.

Through the lesbian and gay experience
　　we may come to desire a new norm for everyone:
We want to make the world more gay
　　(well, at least in its older meaning).
We want to change the shape of the patriarchal table,
　　and find the greatest variety around it.
We want to bring friendship centre stage in human
　　relationships.
We want to make not-touching the exception rather
　　than the rule.

It is only relatively recently that ordinary people
   have begun to have a handle on history,
   the beginnings of access to the levers of power.
Institutions *can* now change.

In the time of Jesus,
   people could be kind to individuals
   who were slaves, women, or poor,
   and indeed change their lives
   (so Paul and the slave Philemon).
Even Jesus himself,
   while indicating strongly that women should be
   protected from divorce,
   did not say, as regards the *institution* of marriage,
   that women were to be empowered as equal to men -
   nor could he have changed that institution on his own.
To say that two people became one flesh
   was more about creating a new social unit
   than entering a relationship of personal mutuality.

And to read from the Gospels
   that the poor will always be with us
   is not to justify structures of oppression.
Perhaps we are now realizing
   that it is the fault of the powerful and wealthy,
and that those structures can be changed.

So the law can change too for lesbian and gay people,
   both secular and ecclesiastical,
   away from a focus on sexual acts
   and towards a recognition
   and protection of relationships.

The Gospels are not blueprints but springboards.
For those who have been oppressed
   they provide not muzzles but muscles.

Campaigns by lesbian and gay people are concerned
   not only with an age of consent,

but also with

   freedom from discrimination
      in housing and employment;

   protection under the law
      from crimes of sexual hatred;

   equality under the law
      on all matters to do with sex;

   an educated and sensitive
      police and judiciary;

   the inclusion of positive approaches
      to lesbian and gay relationships
      in education programmes;

   legal recognition of same-sex partnerships,
      not least in respect of
      housing, pensions, taxation, inheritance;

   financial support for
      community organizations
      and AIDS charities.

There is considerable biblical support for such 'rights':

1   An overall framework of social justice is urged.

2   There is a special concern for the vulnerable.

3   Violence is a major sign of human sinfulness.

A society that shuns,
   that treats lesbian and gay people
      as less than fully human,
   is itself less than fully human.
We belong to one another
   always and everywhere simply as human beings.

A society that shuns
   misses the contributions
      that lesbian and gay people can bring.

A mature society

   welcomes its critics - its prophets and 'fools';

   appreciates gentleness and firmness -
      in both men and women;

   recognizes that both men and women
   can be flexible in their behaviour
   and need not be at the mercy either of biology
   or of social convention;

   clips the wings of aggressive predators;

   strengthens bonds of affection wherever they are found;

   balances striving and competition
      with play and friendship;

   extends its households
      and encourages the strengthening of ties between them;

   enjoys non-genital ways of women and men
      relating to each other;

   needs compassion and tenderness
      in caring for the vulnerable.

Idols are not literally images that we bow down to.
They are anything to which
  or anyone to whom
    we give our allegiance
    in the hope of reward.
They always let us down,
  becoming cruel tyrants over us,
  and when they do we look for someone to blame.

In our society we give our allegiance to
  the market, to money, to possessions;
and we have lost financial security, job satisfaction,
  and full employment.

We also make an idol out of the opposite sex,
  expecting far too much from romantic attachments,
  and also of marriage and family life;
and we have domestic violence, few shared meals,
  and child neglect and abuse.

Who can we blame?

Those who refuse the idols,
  including those who are in creative and caring work,
  usually ill paid or not paid at all,
  and those who do not live in family patterns.

Now *some* gay men (and a few lesbian women)
  opt for a consumer lifestyle
usually those who have a high disposable income,
and *some* lesbian women (and a few gay men)
  opt for a nuclear family life.

Most are either living alternative patterns
  or seeking to do so,
at least to some extent liberated from the idols,
  but constantly threatened by those in thrall to them.

An American writer, Bruce Bawer,
  in a book called A *Place at the Table*,
argued that being homosexual
  should not exclude a person
  from a place at the family table at Thanksgiving.

Fair enough,
  but the people in view in his book
  are mostly male couples in suits
  attending respectable episcopalian churches.
It would be relatively easy for their extended families
  to absorb this slightly different fact about them,
  especially if their tables were labelled 'WASP' -
  White, Anglo-Saxon Protestants.

What if your partner is Jewish?
Or Buddhist?
Or black?
Or the couple are lesbian?

And what is the shape of the table?
  Rectangular?
  The seats at top and bottom with carved arms,
    and the rest with no arms at all?

I want to suggest
  that the gay and lesbian presence
  urges a change,
not simply a personal acceptance,
  but a differently shaped table -

round perhaps?

He was ten years old
  and found himself in purgatory
  on Wednesday afternoons from September to March.
He had to obey the school rules
  and play rugby.
He loathed it,
  and even at that age
  unconsciously tried to change the rules
  by running the wrong way
  just after half-time
  and claiming to have scored a try -
  at the wrong end.
He longed for snow and ice
  so that the game would be cancelled.
But most of the time
  he couldn't escape the social reality
  in which he had for some years to live.
He tried to bluff his way through,
  not to be too near the action to get involved,
  and not too far away to be noticed.
This was not because he was secretly playing
  for the other team,
who would regarded him as much of a hindrance
  as his own,
but out of sheer fright.
Six years later he and the other dregs
  would try to make up their own rules:
'There must be no actual tackling.
  If your opponent courteously taps you on the shoulder,
  you must hand him the ball and say,
  "Certainly. Your turn."
Of course they didn't get far
  and had no desire to invent a new game.
But William Webb Ellis in 1823 started rugby
  by picking up a round ball and running with it.
To make a better game, they changed the shape to oval.
All of which may be a parable.

To be openly gay
  is to be subversive -

of the dis-order of violence,
of a dis-ordered male sexuality,
of marriage as the golden ideal for all,
of the taboos on touch,
  especially on tender touch between men,
of heterosexualiy as a moral and spiritual norm,
of an order that gives men all the power,
of laws about sex dominated by property and inheritance,
of control from the centres of power,
of codes formed solely from so-called sacred texts,
of every institution's inbuilt assumptions
  about superior and inferior people,
of a society governed by rank and domination hierarchies.

The call to people of faith is to be
  tough,
  stern,
  gentle,
  non-violent,
  forgiving
    resisters.

The promise is not of comfort,
  but of justice
  and maybe of glory,
    not the glory of the honours given by worldly powers,
    but the glory of the love shared by transfigured bodies.

The power of money in the struggle for justice:

If you allow a lesbian and gay organization
   to use the cathedral
we will withhold our parish contribution
   to the work of the diocese ...

If we ally ourselves as a women's group
   with lesbian campaigns for justice,
the church will stop our funding ...

If I come out at work,
   I'll lose my job and my income ...

We will fund ambulance services for the suffering
   (counselling and hospices)
but we will not support any campaign
   that wants to change the rule book ...

If I give up the protection of the institution
   and forego the comfort of the regular pay cheque,
there will be a price to be paid ...

You may take away my purse,
   but you cannot take away my freedom ...

If I identify with you,
   I shan't be promoted.

The car?
The holiday?
The pension?

Freedom may be one of our prime spiritual values.
  But is it freedom
    to do what I want?
  Or is that licence?
  And is it freedom
    to act on my human rights?
  Or is that to ignore the rights of others?

Freedom may be worked out in learning how
  to live in communion with others
  and with God,

respecting the dignity and worth of others,
  their boundaries and one's own,
  taking account of how one's actions
    impinge on the territory of others:
  hence the need for good law;

respecting the deeper truths of that love of neighbour,
  which, expressed corporately,
  in the structures and processes of a community,
    is justice.

We need to ask,
  What understanding do we have
    of human identity and dignity?

  In what ways is that understanding
    informed by our religious beliefs,
    for some of us by what we believe we see of God
    in the life of Jesus?

Certain diseases in each generation
　　are overloaded with imported meaning:
AIDS is a prime example in our own time.

At the bio-medical level
　　we can describe the likely consequences
　　　　of HIV infection on the human organism;
　　we now have a range of treatments
　　　　which can at least delay the onset of symptoms;
　　we put considerable resources
　　　　into drugs and vaccines.

At the personal and social level
　　increasing isolation is perhaps
　　　the worst consequence:
　　its features are
　　　　the individual's sense of guilt;
　　　　society's codes of what is shameful
　　　　　　and which therefore leads to rejection,
　　　　　　expressed by pushing away or running away;
　　　　the dynamics of stigma,
　　　　　　which by definition dismisses by category;
　　　　lingering taboos about semen and blood;
　　　　the combination, usually lethal,
　　　　　　of prejudice and ignorance.

At the global level,
　　those most affected by AIDS
　　and least within range of expensive treatments
　　　　are vulnerable populations:
　　the poor, the majority of them non-white;
　　the dispossessed: migrants, refugees, homeless;
　　women in general and prostitutes in particular:
all who have no power to resist the unwanted.
This alerts us to issues of public health and human rights
　　and to the fact that AIDS flourishes
　　where prejudice, ignorance, and poverty combine.

Homosexuality does not cause AIDS:
  HIV infection does.

Prevention is helped by open and relaxed discussion -
  and by advice on safer sex.

HIV can be transmitted by anyone to anyone else
  if either partner has risky sex with others.
No one category of people is more prone than any other -
  except perhaps that lesbian women are least at risk.

We take calculated risks every day,
  driving a car, riding a bicycle, rock climbing.
We therefore have to be discerning where sex is concerned,
  but there will always be risk.
We can never reduce it to zero.
And the law may require us to wear safety belts,
  but who can afford the *extra* safety devices
  urged upon us by a salesman?

There always has been risk.
Sex and death have never been far apart:
  childbirth,
  disease.
There is always the paradox that something that brings
  pleasure, celebration, and exploration
also brings
  pain, restriction, and danger.
There is always the question,
  What limits are prudent - and even wise?
  What limits have been constructed out of fear
    and can be transcended?
A new disease makes us ask ourselves
  about those we wish to draw close to:
Why do I draw close?
How do I draw close?
What are the consequences of drawing close?

Education can persuade.
Treatments can cure or ease.
Vaccines can prevent.
Condoms can lessen risk.
Laws rarely deter,
    but can help exclude overt prejudice or hatred.
In extremis, emergency laws can quarantine ...

Cancer is both disease
    (uncontrollable multiplication of takeover cells)
and illness
    (a social phenomenon needing political action
     against smoking, radiation, and noxious environments).
This second level is ignorable
    if the disease can be blamed entirely on individual choice.

Certain activities can make us more prone to disease:
    drinking to cirrhosis of the liver,
    smoking to lung cancer,
    unprotected sex to HIV and AIDS,
    overwork to stress and heart attacks.
Blame is never apportioned equally.

AIDS has evoked courage, compassion,
    and patient enduring love.
But that does not justify it:
    it remains an offence,
    not least because of so much meaningless suffering.
To God: J'accuse.

Treatments and vaccines eventually take the terror
    out of diseases,
with the consequence that individuals need no longer
    fear isolation and ostracism.

If there is ice on the pavement
  you walk carefully, watching your step.
If there is deep snow on the path
  (or shifting sand or sliding mud)
  you trudge along with effort, with heavy step.
You may well miss your footing and fall over.
When the way is clear, the pavement firm,
  you step out with ease and confidence.

Growing up gay can feel like walking on ice.
Living with AIDS can feel like walking through deep snow.

Those living with AIDS
   can find parallels with the story of Jesus in Gethsemane:

Loneliness as you face your destiny ...

The sleep of those you thought you could count on ...

The desperate plea that it will all go away ...

The delivery to the power(s) of death by intimacy ...

The inability to *do* anything ...

Walking on to greet death with acceptance,
   however hard the dying ...

The possibility of a movement
   from victim to victor,
   from oppressed to free,
   from survivor to thriver ...

Source: Michael Seán Paterson, *Singing for our Lives*, Cairns Publications with Arthur James Ltd, 1997, p. 50, with acknowledgment.

AIDS challenges us to deepen our understanding of

1 the Kingdom of God as the domain
   of the oppressed and outcast:
   its table welcomes the maimed,
   the homeless, the stigmatized:
   its values impel us to struggle for justice.

2 incarnation as central to our understanding of God,
   that the divine is in pain and darkness:
   and that impels us to get involved
   and to be willing to be contaminated;
   as samples of this,
   sexuality and politics are messy, incomplete,
   and always a struggle.

3 the image of God in every human being
   that demands dignity and respect,
   and especially for the despised:
   there is no room for condescension,
   moralizing, or patronizing.

4 the intimacy and warmth
   that we are all seeking to give and receive,
   and that therefore should be characteristic of our care.

5 the need not to rush into words,
   to be reduced (or is it raised?) to silence,
   avoiding glib clichés,
   accepting powerlessness, doubt, ambivalence.

Source: Kenneth Leech, 'The AIDS crisis and pastoral care: some wider implications', a talk given at Nashotah House, Wisconsin, 1986, with acknowledgment.

13
DREAMING AND HOPING

That'll be the day!

An extract from a psychological journal:

Patterns of sexual behaviour are varied.
Do not assume that a person is heterosexual
    because he or she is currently in a relationship
    with a member of the opposite sex.
It may be just a phase.

That'll be the day!

From an advertisement for a crack army regiment:

Gay couples are particularly welcome to apply.
Our experience has shown
   that they encourage each other
   to greater loyalty and bravery
than is shown by most soldiers.

That'll be the day!

An MI5 memo:

Gay and lesbian people in the Secret Services
   will not be discriminated against
   provided they are open about their sexuality
   and relationships
and are therefore not vulnerable to blackmail,
   whether financial or emotional.

NB

We recognize the difference between
   'secret' and 'private':
In this instance we do not ask for secrecy
   and we respect privacy.

That'll be the day!

A member of an interviewing panel for psychiatric nurses:

We find it hard not to discriminate in favour
   of gay and lesbian applicants,
for they consistently demonstrate
   a maturity and sensitivity
   greater than do their heterosexual counterparts.
They know only too well the dangers of a split life
   and of self-hatred,
and how they can lead to mental breakdown.

That'll be the day!

A bishop:

I have no hesitation in appointing
   an openly gay or lesbian presbyter
   to be vicar of a parish.
However, knowing how lonely a life that can be,
   I should prefer to appoint a gay couple
   to share the leadership of the church there -
   or at least to be assured that the vicar concerned
   has a partner sharing the vicarage.
Jesus showed wisdom and sensitivity
   when he sent his followers out two by two,
and in the early days of the Salvation Army
   I gather that officers were always appointed in pairs.
Not that they were all gay or lesbian, of course.
   In a way, that's irrelevant.
But if they happen to be,
   then I can usually assume that they get on well -
and I have noticed that they are often spiritually
   more alert and mature than most heterosexual vicars.

That'll be the day!

The senior partner in a medical practice:

We *must* have someone lesbian or gay
  to replace Chris.
He/she (!) was so good at making sure
    that anxious teenagers who are bothered
    about their homosexual feelings
never came back for a second consultation.
I've never known anyone more able
  to convince people that they weren't ill.

That'll be the day!

A *representative of the current 'moral majority'*:

We were wrong.

That'll be the day!

The principal of a college of education to a student:

Thank you for telling me that you are gay.
I appreciate the trust you have placed in me.
I will write an even better reference for you
    than I was going to do.
Your unusual courage and honesty
    may do something to make up for what is often lacking
    in the staff room.

That'll be the day!

A young curate:

Of course!
  Homosexuality is much more the institution's problem
  than it is mine.
I refuse to let it stop me from making relationships.
I don't think I'm called to be celibate,
  and I don't want to live in a community,
  which is the only safeguard that prevents celibacy
  from being inhuman and making people crabby.
I have no need to live out other people's fears.

That'll be the day!

From a report of the Samaritans:

Of the reasons given by people who have attempted
   to take their own lives,
that of homosexuality shows a dramatic drop
   from the figures five years ago.
The greater acceptance of gay and lesbian people,
   both by themselves of themselves
   and by society as a whole,
has probably done much
   to keep them away from the borders of despair.

That'll be the day!

God:

I've been tempted to give up Project Earth recently,
and turn my attention to a less ambitious scheme.
But gay and lesbian people have put new heart in me.
They are showing up a lot of married couples,
   loving one another in a way
   that echoes deep inside me -
without controlling or possessing
   or manipulating or using violence.
They have been exploring the ways of loving
   with great courage,
and they have stopped trivialising themselves.
Perhaps I'm on the right lines after all ...

INDEX

The words 'gay' and 'lesbian' are not indexed. Whilst many pages are not exclusively of significance to lesbian and gay people, all of them may have some connection.

INDEX

INDEX

INDEX